About the author

My name is Wynn Johnson. I was born on the 28th day of June 1954, in the coal mining region of southeast Kentucky. In birth order, I was number eight of a family of thirteen. We were poor, but we had lots of fun as a family. I grew up in the small village of Weeksbury. It was a place with towering mountains and changing seasons. We had endless room to run. In fact, we had the entire Appalachia mountain range for a playground. It was a place where morals and honesty were taught at home and in school. Two of the most valuable lessons I learned there were the value of learning and the joy of reading.

However, looking out from the lofty peaks of the Cumberland Plateau only created a curiosity within me to find what lay beyond that next set of mountains. I have spent most of my life exploring the Earth and I have read thousands of books along the way. As I have written in previous books, I believe that, if we could eliminate hunger and illiteracy, other problems would disappear. I believe the answer to any question, or the solution to any problem, can be found on the pages of a book.

TALES OF THE MOON

Wynn Johnson

TALES OF THE MOON

Vanguard Press

VANGUARD PAPERBACK

© Copyright 2019
Wynn Johnson

The right of Wynn Johnson to be identified as author of this work has been asserted by him in accordance with the Copyright, Designs and Patents Act 1988.

All Rights Reserved

No reproduction, copy or transmission of this publication may be made without written permission.
No paragraph of this publication may be reproduced, copied or transmitted save with the written permission of the publisher, or in accordance with the provisions of the Copyright Act 1956 (as amended).

Any person who commits any unauthorised act in relation to this publication may be liable to criminal prosecution and civil claims for damages.

A CIP catalogue record for this title is available from the British Library.

ISBN 978 1 784655 93 8

*Vanguard Press is an imprint of
Pegasus Elliot MacKenzie Publishers Ltd.*
www.pegasuspublishers.com

First Published in 2019

**Vanguard Press
Sheraton House Castle Park
Cambridge England**

Printed & Bound in Great Britain

Dedication

Writing a book is a lot of fun, but it's also a lot of work. No one who has ever written a book can say, with honesty, that they did it all by themselves. There are lots of people who play a part in producing books, and I hope I don't forget anyone. First, I want to thank everyone who has read my previous books. It's hard to describe the elation and the honor I felt when the first person read my first book. I still feel the same with each new reader.

Once again, as before, the first person who read this book as a manuscript was Katy Newton Stein. Katy is an avid reader and it meant so much to get her thumbs up.

There are also those who played a personal, and hands-on part in this book. I would like to thank Judith Palmateer, the publisher of my first book. I want to thank my sweetheart and personal adviser, Jessica Stockwell. And once again, I want to thank Jamie Fischer, who has always been a help and a motivator. As I finished each chapter, Jamie read and gave valuable input. My sincere appreciation for my lovely granddaughter, Cassie Roberts for her amazing photography skills. She combined three different photos from three phases of the moon, to create this wonderful book cover.

A heart-felt thanks to Suzann Mulvey, Jenna Evans and all the people at Pegasus.

Tales of the Moon is a story of adventure, with a touch of horror and mystery. Based on true life events, it follows a young man through ever changing times and places, during the course of nearly forty years. Sometimes happy, sometimes sad. If you enjoy adventure, you'll love *Tales of the Moon*.

Chapter One

I admit it, I was a pretty dumb kid. I marveled at everything I saw from the time I was able to see. I was born in the mid-1950s to a large family in southeast Kentucky. It's a beautiful place today, but even more so back then. The old house stood in a clearing, with a barn and pasture which totaled about ten acres, deep in the head of a hollow. Counting the uncleared portion, the farm totaled almost three hundred acres. Beyond the pasture was dense forest and steep mountainsides in every direction. There was a creek that flowed past the house and I just couldn't help wondering where all that water was coming from. When I was old enough to walk I would sneak out of the house. I knew I wasn't supposed to, but it became a daily quest for new adventure. I ventured a little further each day and each time I was caught, scolded, and reminded of the horrors lurking just beyond the pasture.

The scolding didn't seem to be any more severe, whether I only went a little way or if there had to be an all-out search to find me. Make no mistake, you could get your bottom warmed in those days and I often did. But I soon realized I could survive that as well.

One day I wandered all the way to the barn and ducked out of sight, but I still couldn't see where that water was coming from. This time I was caught red-handed by an older brother, so I thought I would soften the consequences if I started a conversation. "Where's all that water coming from?" I asked.

My brother responded, "Lots of places, fool. Now come on. You're going to get snake bite wandering around by yourself out here." Now that wasn't so bad, but it still didn't answer my question.

That evening I was lectured about the danger of wild animals and snakes. Then I was told what would happen if I died. I would be placed in a box and lowered into a deep dark hole and covered with dirt, never to be seen again. This new fear kept me from wandering, at least for a little while.

Then the trees changed into every beautiful color imaginable. I wondered about that too, but the colorful leaves were soon gone. With no leaves on the trees, I could see the ridgeline and that really amused me. From my perspective, it looked as if someone were to climb to the top, he would fall right down the other side. They looked to be as sharp as the edge of a sheet of paper. I wondered if I could balance myself and walk heel-to-toe along the ridgeline without falling down one side of the mountain or the other.

Then the snow came, and I wondered why it was a stark and boring white. But I soon found it to be cold and unpleasant, so I stayed indoors and wondered why the fire was hot.

Being inside with my older siblings that winter gave me the opportunity to ask questions, and so I did. One explanation only led to another question. Then came the first spring of my memory and a whole new set of things to wonder about. You see, there were a lot of fruit trees and spring flowers. So why was this one white and why was that one pink?

I watched people dig in the dirt and drop in seeds and I wondered why. And there was that creek again and even more water than there had been before. I just had to know where all that water was coming from, so I headed upstream. The farm animals watched as I walked past them. They looked at me almost as if they knew I was not supposed to be wandering off alone.

The barn was the first phase of my journey. I stopped for several long minutes, looking around cautiously, for this was where I had been captured the last time. I held my breath and all I heard was the sounds of the birds and animals, so I ventured onward. I crawled under the fence and looked back again. Still no one in sight.

The stream had created a dark green tunnel through the forest, but there was a narrow footpath along the side. I stumbled along the path another one hundred yards or so then stopped, completely confused. The stream split, and I wasn't sure what to do. I turned to look back toward home. Sure, looked like a long way back. I thought I'd better turn back and think about it for a while. I felt good about the fact that I had not been caught. I would retrace my steps to the back yard, innocently play there for a while then duck through the kitchen door as if I had never been anywhere. As I turned, I tripped over my own feet and fell headlong into the coldest water I had ever felt. This left me with only one thing to do and that was to let out a long and mournful scream. I saw my mother and older sister coming at full speed, red-faced and frightened out of their wits. I knew there would be consequences this time.

But the penalty wasn't nearly bad enough to stop my exploring, so the next time I went even further. Just as my brother had told me, the stream split again and again, apparently it was coming from everywhere. The streams led me further and further up the mountain. Looking straight across to the next, and closest, mountain, I could tell that I was almost halfway to the top. Assuming the two mountains were the same height. So, would I dare to go even higher, knowing I was already walking on forbidden ground? Of course, I just had to go further.

Just then I heard a voice in the distance calling my name and I knew it would be a dead giveaway if I answered. So, I dashed back down the mountain following the stream. If I got back quick enough I would get away with it, but there was the voice again. My mother had already searched the barn and she was just coming out as I was crawling under the fence. This time the lecture was about mountain lions, bears and snakes that could kill a person with one bite. The lecture stopped my expeditions for a while, but not my curiosity.

The leaves changed colors again, fell to the ground, exposing the mountaintop again. By now I had lost my fascination with the stream. I would ignore the creek and head straight up the mountain as fast as I could go. This time I would see what was at the top, come what may. Just when I was sure I couldn't go any further, the steep mountainside became a gentle slope, then flat. At last, there I was standing dead center of the ridgeline. I took a moment to catch my breath, then I looked around.

The only word that escaped me was wow. There was a whole new world out there. Mountains, mountains and more mountains as far as I could see. I walked to where the mountain began to drop down the other side. From there I could see a new valley. Far below, to the left and about half way down, a patch of fog floated slowly to the left. To the right, and deep in the valley, I could see another creek. A creek much larger than one near my home. There was also a road and some houses. The ground I stood on was brown and yellow with autumn leaves. However, the mountains in the distance were a smoky blue in color.

Another spring came, and I continued my exploration, picking flowers for my mother as a peace offering. As I grew, my eldest sister complained that to find me, the only thing she had to do was look for my almost white head of hair sticking up out of the weeds. There were no dwarf fruit trees in those days. Most fruit trees grew tall and strong, like any other tree.

In the spring when the apple trees were in bloom I would climb as high as I could, where I would marvel at the colors. The bright green leaves, the white and pink blossoms and the deep blue sky above it all captivated me for hours. I peeked into birds' nests, at the blue robin eggs, the brown speckled eggs of the brown thrush, and the hanging baskets of the wren. I was growing and learning, but everything around was confusing to me.

When the hunting dogs were available I took them along to ward off snakes and other monsters. I learned to recognize the difference in the dog's bark. Dogs barking at a rabbit was a totally different sound than dogs barking at a snake. When there was more growl than bark, it was without a doubt a snake. The next question would be, was it a harmless black racer, or a deadly copperhead?

I learned to carry a walking stick and to be deadly accurate at throwing stones. This was the most effective way to deal with snakes. I also learned to kill the snake first, then figure out whether it was poisonous or not. I also had to convince myself I wasn't afraid of snakes even though they terrified me.

I was beginning to realize how large the Earth must be and how little of it I was seeing. As painful as it was for me, I knew I had to grow and to learn. Then when the time was right, I would see the world.

My brother had lost an eye while playing with a pocket knife. The closest optometrist was located about fifty miles away in the city of Hazard. My brother had to be taken to see that doctor repeatedly during the first year after the accident. One day I was allowed to ride along. I was fascinated by the lights, the buildings, the neon signs and the traffic. Cars, pickup trucks, large trucks, and buses. And there were so many different colors.

Throughout my life, I found it impossible not to wonder and to ask why. Someone once tried to teach me to meditate. "Relax," she told me. "Don't think about anything, and you won't even know where the time went."

Nope. Sorry, I just couldn't do it. There are too many things happening in the world.

Looking back at my childhood memories, it's like looking at someone else's life. I'm sixty-three now, and I have to say, I have no regrets. It's been a wonderful life. I just wish I could have lived it a little slower. I wish there had been a rewind button to go back, pause and enjoy the good times. I wish there had been a fast-forward button to hurry through the long days of sorrow. Someone once told me that life is like a roll of toilet paper. The closer you get to the end, the faster it goes, and it all goes down the drain. A clever way of putting it, but it's true. I shouldn't complain, my life has been better than most, and longer than many. But I'll tell you one thing, my life has been a wondrous journey. And the people along the way made it all worth living.

Chapter Two

I guess you could have called Weeksbury a town, but the folks there called it a coal camp. In its heyday, it was a bustling place with various stores and shops. It was coal that made the wheels of the area turn. The earth would often rumble as blasting occurred deep underground or on the mountainsides. Small streams flowed from mine openings as underground aquifers were drained. There was a constant earthy smell due to ongoing excavation. Roads were often rutted and muddy, but it was home.

Weeksbury was a fun place to grow up. There was a time between wars when the world seemed to be at peace. The 1950s, and early 1960s, were a time of new and exciting things. Horror movies and science fiction movies were shown at the theatre at Wheelwright and at the drive-in theatres at Martin, Prestonsburg and Pikeville. We all knew that Weeksbury was, to say the least, behind the times. Movies were usually old news by the time they made it to our local screens. But that, too, added to the peaceful innocence of Eastern Kentucky.

It was a time when we did not yet know what was on the moon and we certainly didn't know whether or not there was life on Mars. We still lived with the possibility of an invasion from outer space. We lived with the possibility that nuclear testing could cause an octopus to grow into a gigantic monster large enough to destroy the Golden Gate Bridge. That innocence kept us young and the world around us fascinating. I don't think we wanted to know the harsh reality of the outside world. It was far more fun to imagine and to be mystified.

Seasons passed amazingly fast. Cold, swollen streams gushed from the mountainsides with the melting snow in the spring. People worked to clear last year's dead weed stems and cornstalks from their gardens. All this debris was raked to the downhill side of the garden and burned. The smell of the burning stalks would fill the air, and it was a pleasant smell. A smell that will stay with me forever. Folks back then didn't know of the environmental damage caused by the smoke and the fire. How could they have known?

There were sounds of men shouting commands to their work horses in early spring. Before you knew, the fields were green, and the sun was hot. But I swear to you I can remember days that were so perfect. It was as if the beauty of heaven had spilled down to sprinkle over the earth. Leaves were dark green in June, and there were morning glories everywhere, with large dark green leaves and multicolored blossoms. There were lots of wild flowers, but the morning glories with their rich and multiple colors has always been a favorite among Kentucky folks. When July rolled around, it was almost as if someone closed a water faucet. The rains would suddenly stop, and the weather would become hot, and humid.

Electric trolleys pulled coal from the mines and along mountainside roads where the coal was dumped into what was called a tipple. To drive the trolley, the driver would touch a cable/conductor to a high voltage line that was strung on poles above the track. This would create a bright white flash that could be seen for miles. Folks called the flashes motor arcs. On hot summer nights, those motor arcs were often mistaken for lightning. We wanted the lightning. Just a thunderstorm to cool a sweltering night. And, sometimes, it was lightning. The rain would beat hard on the roof of that old house, and a cool wind would blow through the open windows. That cool breeze would knock me out cold. The next day, I couldn't have told you whether it rained all night or only for a few minutes.

Showers would occur more frequently in August when we got what the old folks called, Dog Day Showers so named for the Dog Star. Even though the Dog Star can only be seen during the winter, in the northern hemisphere. Regardless of what they were called, the showers were a welcome and temporary relief from the summer heat. But when the showers had passed, the heat and humidity were even more unbearable.

There was a tall walnut tree that stood high on a steep bluff, not far from the house. The fact that the tree stood high on the hill made it look as if it stretched right into the clouds. A cool wind would begin to blow just before one of those late August showers. The first bright yellow leaves would blow from the top of that walnut tree and drift slowly into the yard. We played a game as children when those leaves fell. The one who caught the most leaves in mid-air would one day be rich, and prosperous. We pretended the leaves were gold dust falling from the heavens.

School would start the first week in September when the weather was still hot. The school had no air conditioning, and we sat in class and dreamed of the cooler days of autumn. We dreamed of winter, and sledding down steep, snowy hills. But the autumn days would come, and they were too few, the winter days would come, and they were too cold. You know, it's funny how we're never happy with what nature gives us.

We learned to notice the tell-tale signs of autumn. There was an eerie stillness over the mountain tops, and dense morning fog settled over the low lands. We noticed the silence of the birds, and their flocking for migration. We noticed the wilted summer flowers, the brown leaves that had stressed and fallen in the shorter days. Such a bitter-sweet time of year, a time when things die or sleep for such a long time.

There was however, a time of bliss in September and October. Kids played baseball till the season ended, then basketball and football through the winter. Kids celebrated and cheered with every win. Pretty, young girls became cheerleaders, while the not so pretty ones sat on the sidelines with envy. But all the kids sobbed and mourned over one silly moment when the ball didn't fall through the hoop, or the football didn't pass between goal posts.

We each had our own dreams, as for my brothers and I, it happened to be baseball. My brother Charles and I would get off the bus at the mouth of the hollow and walk home. I guess it was about a half mile. We'd play pass with a baseball as we walked home. If a downhill pass was missed, the ball would roll a hundred yards or so back down the road, and one of us had to go after it.

It was peak season for baseball as major league teams fought their way to the World Series in October. Charles and I never missed a game. Basketball and football seasons were underway, and it seemed the entire world watched or played. Like everyone else, we had our own dreams.

Chapter Three

The population of Weeksbury in 1960 was about a thousand and some odd few. And it was that odd few who kept things interesting. There were my Uncles Ivan and Harold, and a cousin Burlen who were in a constant state of mischief. They also had an uncanny way of getting away with it. John Ray owned a little store near the mouth of Shop Hollow. It was a small building where he sold pop, candy, bread, lunch meat and some canned goods. Now the three in question had been eyeing this target for some time and they were sure John's prices were way too high. One night after the moon had sunk below the mountain they went to work. Using a log and a twenty-foot section of steel rail they raised one corner of the building enough to crawl under and remove some flooring.

They packed everything they could carry into burlap sacks and headed down the road. What they didn't realize, was that one of the sacks had a hole in it, spilling a trail of evidence. Weeksbury was asleep at that time of night. But to be on the safe side they decided they had better get out of town. So, they doubled back and doubled the evidence along the way. One of the Newsome boys looked out the window and saw the outlaws passing on the road in front of their house. He was just too sleepy to go out to investigate, but it just didn't look right to him. In the meantime, the three robbers cut through a pasture and into the tall timber where the evidence trail ended. They took their ill-gotten booty to their favorite camping spot at Collier Rocks where they had a feast.

The Newsome boys we called The Cartwrights, from the TV show Bonanza. The TV show was about a father and his three sons. One of those sons got himself in trouble in every episode for something that wasn't his fault. It was much the same for the Newsome boys. At least one of them would find himself in the wrong place at the wrong time.

In the Newsome family, Frank was the father. He was a hard-working coal miner, and their mother (Agnes) was a stay at home mom. Frank and Agnes had four boys and no girls. Doug was the eldest, followed by Darrel, Bill and Tommy. They were good boys, but they too were prone to a little mischief.

It was not quite daylight when Tommy woke up and went out to the road to solve the mystery of the travelers who passed in the night. He just couldn't believe his eyes. He ran back into the house to enlist the help of his brothers. "A treasure," he told them. And with that, the four of them followed the treasure trail. There was spearmint gum, Juicy Fruit gum, Mars Bars and Milky Way. They were sure it was a gift from the heavens. After they had gathered everything they could find, they hid their treasure in the cellar and swore an oath not to tell a soul. Then they went back to bed.

Mid-morning, they awoke to the sound of voices outside the house. They didn't think much of it when they saw both their parents talking to John Ray and Floyd County sheriff Joe Wheeler Louis in front of the house. The sheriff said, "John's store was robbed last night."

Agnes said, "Well don't think it was my boys. They went to bed early and they're still in bed."

Just then Darrel came out stretching, yawning and already chewing gum. The sheriff said to him, "Hey, Darrel! Can I have a word with you?"

Darrel walked lazily over and said, "What can I do for you, sheriff? I was out late last night, and I got up way too early this morning."

The sheriff asked, "Darrel, where did you get that gum?"

Darrel pulled a pack from his pocket and offered the sheriff the entire pack, and said, "Just keep the whole pack, we've got plenty." The investigation ended, then and there. Frank paid John for his damages.

Before I continue with the capers of our three bandits, I'll have to give you a lengthy description of their next set of victims. George and Caroline Tackett were an elderly couple who lived in a small log cabin on the other side of the mountain, at the headwaters of Long Fork Creek. They married young and had always lived a secluded life, a pioneer life if you will. They knew nothing of the modern world, and didn't care to learn. Talk about superstitious.

They wouldn't set fence posts when the moon was full, for fear that a full moon was much heavier, and its gravity would pull the posts from the ground. They tilled the ground, planted their seeds and harvested their crops according to the *Farmers' Almanac*, and that was the only modern tool they needed. They believed that hanging a dead snake from a tree would cause rain to fall until the snake was removed.

Early in the century when automobiles were becoming popular, they were especially so among salesmen. Selling fruit in an area where fruit trees were plentiful was like trying to sell ice to the Eskimo. But, that's exactly what a salesman attempted to do when he visited George and Caroline, in the summer of 1910.

Loaded heavily with apples, the young man went roaring and bouncing up the bumpy, washed out lane toward the Tackett's cabin. It was a day when some cars didn't have tops, and the driver sat on them, versus in them. And cars were guided with a stick versus a steering wheel.

Caroline saw the man coming and was terrified. She yelled, "Great Scott, George! What is that thing coming up the road?" George took one look and headed out the door with his shotgun to defend their home. He ran to meet the man and his car, and with no word of warning, he blasted the car dead in the radiator. The salesman didn't wait for George to reload, he jumped from the car and headed for the tall timber. The old car drifted off the lane and into a tree where it sat, steaming. George returned to the house and placed his shotgun in a corner. Caroline asked, "Did you kill that thing, George?"

George said, "No, but I made it turn that man lose."

The closest grocery store was Hulbert Mullet's in Weeksbury. This was about a five-mile trek for them and they made it on foot, every Friday morning. They followed a trail that led through a low pass, known as John Gap.

George and Caroline became victims of the robbers and their pranks. There were plenty of places to hide along the trail to execute their evil deeds. There were plenty of snakes to be had in the area as well. The bandits killed one every week and placed it in the path. They would tie a string to the snake's tail and when the two approached they pulled the snake slowly backward. This didn't frighten George and Caroline. However, they did spin tales of mysterious, backward-crawling snakes.

The ultimate prank was the day they tied an empty sugar sack to a long pole. As the old couple walked slowly past they lit their torch and set fire to the sack George was carrying on his back. It started as a small flame at first, and went unnoticed as the couple walked on. The old couple didn't notice the fire until the contents of the sack had spilled to the ground. By then the three bandits were long gone.

Another of their antics was freeing livestock. Unless a barn door or gate had an honest to goodness lock, whatever was inside a fence or barn was set free. Not all animals were let out, some of them were let in. Oscar Thompson and his wife Beedi forgot to lock their kitchen door. They came home to find a full-grown billy goat munching on their new tablecloth. Oscar was not a big man, but he was sure he could handle that goat. He grabbed the goat by the horns, but the goat did not want to go. When it was over, the poor frightened animal had loosed its bowels on the kitchen floor, and a glass china cabinet had been broken.

Then there was Ronnie Skiles and Elmer Spears, who mastered the fine art of stealing chickens. Most chickens in Weeksbury were free-range. This didn't make it easy to steal chickens, but it made it less noticeable. The chicken thieves stole every chicken Lent and Martha Tackett had, except one old rooster.

Ronnie tied a thread to a grain of corn and dropped it in front of the old bird. Ronnie simply walked away dragging the bait, with the old rooster following behind pecking away at the corn. Lent saw the rooster following Ronnie but didn't see the bait. He exclaimed, "Look at this Martha, he's stolen so many chickens he's got them trained to follow him."

The next interesting character was Pete Roberts. The poor guy didn't have a car, or even a driver's license for that matter. He loved his liquor, and everyone knew it. Oh boy, did he ever love his liquor. There were three such individuals in Weeksbury. They were not bad guys. Probably the most heinous crime they ever committed was stealing unguarded pop bottles. They also stole a few fruits and vegetables from time to time, but I don't think they ever graduated to stealing chickens.

It must have been because they were always out walking the roads or hitch-hiking, but for whatever the reason they seemed to be first on the scene of any happening. Such was the case on a Saturday night in 1973, near Wheelwright. Except for Pete Roberts, the names in this story shall remain anonymous.

It all started when an ageing widow found out that worthless son-in-law of hers beat up her daughter. She didn't say much, she just drove to her daughter's home at Burton and shot her son-in-law through the heart. She then got in her car and drove home. Soon afterwards her phone rang. It was her daughter telling her that the dead man's father and brothers were on their way. The old woman locked all the doors and headed for the basement. When the men arrived, they didn't bother knocking. They just bundled twenty sticks of dynamite together and slammed it through her front window, then drove away. They counted on the dynamite to do the trick, but it didn't. You see, the thing about explosives is that it blows up. The force of the explosion blew the house to splinters, leaving nothing but the front door standing. The old lady was sleeping on a cot in the basement when the house went up. She suffered only bruises and punctured eardrums. She would live to face justice. That is if the police ever showed up to arrest her. They were still at the scene of the shooting.

When the first spectators arrived, they found Pete Roberts pounding on what was left of the front door, yelling, "Let me in. I just know somebody's hurt in there." Poor old Pete was too drunk to realize, he could've stepped around the door on either side.

Two young men did just that. They paid no attention to Pete as he continued knocking. They dashed through the rubble, and down the basement steps. They found the old lady dazed, confused and tapping her ears with the palms of her hands, in an attempt to regain her hearing. The two young men carried her up the steps and into the front yard, where the State Police had just pulled in. The officer asked her, "Did you shoot your son-in-law?"

She said loudly, "Huh?"

The officer spoke louder. "Did you shoot your son-in-law?"

The old lady repeated. "Huh! I can't hear you. Somebody blowed up my house."

With that the officer put her in the back of his squad car and took her to Wheelwright. There was a small holding cell at the city hall, so he placed her there and headed off to look for the dynamiters. The problem is that the blasting crew was watching city hall from a distance. They didn't have any more dynamite, but they had a siphoning hose. They stole enough gasoline out of the fire truck to burn down the city hall, including the fire truck. Good citizens arrived and rescued the old lady just in time. She was then taken to Pikeville and placed in jail.

The Pike County sheriff came in on Monday morning and said. "We can't hold her here. This crime took place in Floyd County. She's going to have to be taken to Prestonsburg." She was only in the Prestonsburg jail overnight when the father of the dead man walked in with a handful of money to pay her bail. He told her as she was walking out. "The only reason I bailed you out is, so I can kill you." With that, the sheriff arrested the bailor, but after a mental evaluation, he too was released.

Pete was a harmless fellow, and everyone knew it. Folks who saw him out walking didn't hesitate to pick him up and take him home. Jimmy Little picked him up one day walking through the rain near the top of Abner Mountain. On this day Pete smelled of liquor but didn't appear to be intoxicated. He climbed into the back seat and talked about the weather. He then proceeded to talk about hunting, and about days gone by. In every sense of the word, he appeared to be as sober as a nun.

From the main road in Weeksbury, Pete lived in a small house on the other side of the creek. There was also a gravel road, and the railroad track, but the distance was less than a hundred yards. The creek was a fast flowing one where workers had built stone walls on each side to prevent erosion. The bridge crossing the creek was not a footbridge, it was built for cars. It was a full twelve feet wide, with an iron railing on either side, with the bridge deck about ten feet above the water. Jimmy offered to drive Pete across the bridge to his home.

Pete said, "No, Jimmy. You've done enough. I'll hoof it from here." With that, he stepped out of the car and made a beeline for the bridge and missed it. There was a splash, and by the time Jimmy got to where he could see him, he had washed downstream a short distance. He had pulled himself onto the bank where he lay on his back weeping. Pete was crying, "I broke it. I broke it, I just know it's broke."

Jimmy asked him, "Did you break your leg, Pete?" He said, "No, I broke my liquor."

One morning an ambulance went roaring through Weeksbury. One of the other town drunks I mentioned earlier was found dead at fifty-one years of age. Since I can't think of one bad thing to say about him, I guess I'll at least reveal his first name (Ovie). The fact is, Ovie had a lot of friends. Del Marion and company handled the funeral services. Visitation and viewing would be at the First Baptist Church of Weeksbury.

It's customary to hold church services for about three days, (the number of days from the crucifixion to the resurrection). It's also a custom that the body never be left alone during those days. Pete Roberts and Elmer Spears volunteered to do the overnight duty at the church. Ben Mullet and his wife thought it would be a nice gesture to take sandwiches and coffee to the graveyard shifters. Driving up Number One Road they met Pete and Elmer going in the opposite direction, running for their lives.

Before they could ask them why, Pete and Elmer ran past them. Ben had to turn the car around and chase them down. When Ben caught up with them he asked if something went bump in the night at the old church. Elmer said, "It went bump, it moaned, it groaned, and we're never setting foot in that place again; not even in the daytime."

Ben said, "Maybe it was the pipes."

Pete said, "I don't care if that ghost does smoke a pipe, we're not going back there." Everyone had a laugh at the expense of the two guardians, but no one volunteered to do the overnight shift. Ovie was buried the next morning.

Elmer lived in a row of houses high above the village on what was known as Yellow Flat. From there he could see what was being called The Mysterious Johnson Cemetery Light. It was a pale, white light that could be seen from dusk to dawn, eerily fading in and out. They first noticed the strange phenomenon, shortly after Ovie's funeral. Pete and Elmer were certain it was the spirit of Ovie, waving from the grave. Stranger still, Ovie was not buried on the Johnson Cemetery.

The mystery continued, and a lot of good ghost-fearing citizens began to believe it. It seemed, however, that no one was willing to investigate. One evening Jimmy Johnson asked Pete and Elmer if either of them had ever gone to the cemetery to see what it was. Of course, they wanted no part of any such investigation. Anyway, it never seemed to leave the cemetery, so they thought it best to let sleeping ghosts lie.

The cemetery was a mile or so from Yellow Flat and about half way up Shop Hollow. Two of my brothers, Jimmy and Charles, just couldn't take it any more, they went to investigate. Sure enough, the mystery light appeared at dusk. It was pale at first, then became brighter as the night grew darker. As the two approached the cemetery they realized the eerie light was shining from a specific grave. As they fought their way through the weeds and the myrtle vines they noticed that the light was in fact fading in and out. Suddenly, the mystery was solved. The light was nothing but the glow of an outdoor light reflecting in a polished granite tombstone. The fading in and out occurred when a tall poplar tree swayed in the breeze blocking the glow. The only irony is that the light was a mercury-type, dusk to dawn light, shining from Elmer's own brother Bill's house next door to his own.

Chapter Four

That brings me to our next Weeksbury subject. Let me see if I can figure out a way to describe Paul Eddie Lackey. You've seen the way a rowdy kitten runs through the house looking for something to get in to. And while you're cleaning up one mess, the kitten makes another. That's the only way I know of describing Paul Eddie Lackey. He honestly did not see himself as mischievous. However, he would labor long into the wee hours of the morning to put long wood screws in the outhouse doors at church.

He had an old green car, about a 1951, Buick. I'm not sure it belonged to him, I think he just found it somewhere and the owner didn't care that he took it. I mean, the thing didn't even have a motor in it. Both of Weeksbury's roads were uphill from the entrance of town to dead ends. Paul Eddie would gather the neighborhood kids and they would push that old car as far as they could, then jump in and ride it back down again. Someone asked if he ever intended to put an engine in it and he said, "No, it would be too hard to push with a big old heavy motor in it."

If someone's cat showed up with paper boots, or a dog with tin cans tied to its tale, the entire world looked at Paul Eddie Lackey. One stormy night, just after midnight there was a loud knock at Jack and Thelma Mullet's door. Jack was a retired coal miner, he was as good natured as anyone could be. He was also a no-nonsense kind of fellow.

Still half asleep he wondered if there had really been a knock at the door, so he waited and listened until the knock sounded again. Something had to be terribly wrong if someone was out on such a stormy night, so he rushed to the door. There was Paul Eddie soaked to the skin wearing an old hat that looked as if it had melted down over his head. To soften the conversation, he called him Uncle Jack, and he said to him, "Uncle Jack, can you give me a push?"

Jack said, "No I won't give you a push. It's one in the morning, and the rain is pouring." With that, Jack closed the door and returned to bed.

Thelma asked, "Who was it, honey?"

Jack said, "It was Paul Eddie. He wanted me to give him a push, that old car of his must be in the ditch."

Thelma asked, "Well are you going to help him?"

Jack said, "Thelma, it's one in the morning and the rain is pouring."

Thelma said, "Oh bless his heart. He tries so hard. And besides, Jack. Don't you remember when those young men helped us when we were stuck on Buckingham Mountain?"

Jack went to the closet and put on his raincoat and hat. He didn't even stop at the front porch he just strolled right out into the rain, eager to get it over with. But he didn't see Paul nor his car, so he yelled into the night, "Paul! Paul! Are you still out here?"

Paul yelled back, "Yeah!"

Jack asked, "Do you still need a push?"

Paul yelled back, "Yeah!"

Jack said, "Well, where are you? I can't see you."

Paul yelled back, "I'm in the swing!" Like so many people in that area, Paul Eddie Lackey faded from the picture. But there were plenty of Weeksbury subjects to take his place.

Truman Tackett drove a hearse for Del Marion Funeral services for many years. However, Truman developed a long-term illness and was unable to work for several months. Del was forced to hire another driver. Del wanted to do something for Truman, so he sold him the hearse he had driven for so long at a very reasonable price. So, Truman created the East Kentucky Taxi Cab Company. Since there was no other taxi service within a hundred miles, he knew he would have a corner on the market.

Word spread fast and Truman was ready for his first customer, who happened to be Hazel Vanover. She climbed into the backseat and they were off to Martin. As they approached Vicars Service Station, she said to him, "Truman, can we stop here for a moment, I need a pack of cigarettes." Truman was a little hard of hearing, so they continued down Highway 122 toward Martin. Ten minutes later they were approaching Russell Sloan's station. This time she would make sure Truman heard her, so she leaned forward and tapped him lightly on the right shoulder. Truman hit the brakes, swerved to the right, down over a small embankment; only to be stopped by a patch small trees. Neither of them was hurt and the car was not damaged. Hazel said to him, "Gee, Truman, I really didn't mean to startle you."

He said, "You know, twenty years of driving this thing and that's the first time a customer spoke to me from the back."

Another story he liked to tell was the Sunday morning when he took Fanny Blankenship to Pikeville to see a friend at the hospital. It's important to describe Fanny to the reader. She was a red-headed lady who looked very much like the country music star, Minnie Pearl. Fanny knew everything about everyone. We had party lines in Weeksbury, and you could not use the phone without asking her for the line. After your call went through you would often hear a click, and Fanny would still be on the line.

They left early on that Sunday morning, and they hadn't gone far when Fanny asked Truman to stop at Vicars gas station. Truman pulled in, but the station was closed. He said, "They're closed, Fanny, maybe the station on the other side of the mountain is open at Indian Creek Junction." Now I wouldn't swear to it, but there's a good possibility that Fanny had a little nip of something before they left for Pikeville.

When they reached the top of Abner Mountain Fanny asked, "So, Truman, do you think that station will be open?"

Truman said, "Well I just don't know, Fanny, it being Sunday and all." It's twelve miles across that mountain, and that's a long way when you have to pee. But Fanny had not told Truman why stopping was so urgent. She drew a deep breath when the sign said, closed Sundays and holidays.

They made it almost to Pikeville when Fanny said, "Truman, you have to stop."

Truman said, "What's wrong, Fanny?"

Fanny said, "I have to pee, that's what's wrong."

Truman stopped the car and Fanny headed downhill toward the river. When she came back she was mad. She jumped into the back seat and slammed the door. She said, "There's just too many people in the world. I was down there peeing, and I looked across the river and there was a man fishing. I had to think fast, I just pulled my dress up over my head to keep him from seeing my face. That way, if he ever sees me again, he won't recognize me."

There was also the antics of the Newsome family. They were wonderful folks, just a little haphazard. When the big coal companies pulled out they left a number of vacant buildings. There were two brick buildings about forty feet wide and one hundred feet long, which stood at the mouth of Shop Hollow. One of these was a machine shop, that was used for repairing mining equipment. The other was a warehouse, which we called the supply house. That building contained everything from administrative supplies to hammers and nails.

Cash money was in short supply during the Second World War, so miners were paid with paper promissory notes called script. These notes could only be redeemed for goods at the company store. Quantities of script was left behind in the supply building. The windows of the buildings were covered with a heavy wire mesh. Mysteriously, one corner of the mesh became undone on one of the supply house windows. And I'm sure it was by some bizarre accident, but the pane in that same window somehow got broken. With large windows on all four sides, the inside of the building was as bright as the day outside. At first there appeared to be nothing of value left behind, but then... Eureka! A full box of script, in denominations of ones, fives, even twenty-dollar bills. Script became the currency of the kids in

Weeksbury, until it was passed around to the point that it was no longer legible.

The older children had a more productive vision for the building. The pine wood floor, and open rafters... You get the picture. The first basketball game was held there in the summer of 1962. Teenagers came for miles around. The games lasted throughout the day on Saturdays and Sundays. This sort of competition was without a doubt the very roots of the greatest college basketball team in the nation. The Kentucky Wildcats.

The last game of the day on a late Sunday afternoon was competition between the Caleb Fork Blue Devils, and the Number One Rattlers. Caleb Fork was represented by Doug, Bill, Darrell, Tommy Newsome and Freddy Lane. The team from Number One was, Marril Little, Johnny Collins, Wayne Joe Burke, Crittenden Sword and Ronnie Skiles.

It was early in the game, and the boys were full of energy. The Caleb boys had openly bragged of Tommy Newsome's jump-shot abilities. About the third time down the court, Tommy went up for his highest jump ever. But what goes up must come down, and down he went, right through the floor and into the basement.

Both teams and all the onlookers rushed down the steps to the fallen player. The sixteen-year-old didn't moan or groan, he screamed, and with good reason. The splintering boards left scrapes, and painful superficial cuts all over the boy's body. But nothing severe, just painful. Doug was the eldest of the boys, so he performed the examination. To know the severity of the injuries, Tommy would have to be stripped. So, they removed his clothing, yep, all his clothing. Doug realized there were too many injuries to be treated in the field. He threw Tommy over his shoulder and headed for home.

Doug paid no attention to the fact that his mother (Agnes) was having an after-church social gathering with a group of ladies. He gently placed Tommy on the floor in the middle of the social circle, in all his glory, and demanded medical attention for him. Agnes realized in an instant there were no severe injuries, and demanded, "You get some clothes on that child."

Doug pointed vehemently and demanded, "Do something for him, he's a bleeding." But Tommy never missed a game. By the following Sunday, the floor of the supply house had been repaired and he was back on the court.

When the boys were older they were allowed to partake in the Sunday afternoon penny poker game in the front yard. All chores and tasks were placed on hold for such an important event. One task that was put on hold that day was feeding the hogs. Late in the afternoon, and several cocktails into the game, a hungry sow and eight piglets found a way out of the pen. Totally immersed in the game were all four boys and Frank, their father. The sow simply grunted a greeting as she walked past the busy game with her family. The only one who seemed to notice was Doug, who looked up and said, "Boys, there she goes."

The chase didn't begin until about an hour later, when the sow and pigs had meandered nearly a quarter of a mile up the mountain. It was a simple plan, they would surround the sow and pigs and drive them slowly, and steadily back to the pen. But an intoxicated person doesn't consider stealth. The instant the sow heard the rovers in the brush, she bolted straight up the mountain, and the pigs scattered in every direction.

Passersby paid little attention to the cursing, rock throwing, and brush thrashing. By sunset the hunt had moved to the next mountain. In the meantime, the sow went back to where the chase had begun. With a few squeals and grunts, she gathered her litter and returned to the pen at feeding time. Elmer Spears happened to be walking by, and saw the animals enter the pen through a hole in the fence. He gathered some boulders and placed them in front of the hole, and as he walked away he saw the beaten and bedraggled round-up crew coming out of the woods. He simply yelled over his shoulder as he walked away, "You all better fix that hole in the fence. Your hogs might get out."

About a hundred and twenty miles away near Huntington West Virginia was an amusement park, known as Camden Park. The Newsome family had seen the park advertised on TV and had wanted to take a family outing at that park for years. Early one Saturday morning they set out. After they passed Prestonsburg, they entered uncharted territory. They got lost. There was plenty of blame and cursing to go around. However, at sundown, they decided to cut their losses and head for home, if they could find home. And they did, they made it in late that night, tired and frustrated. But they were not to be deterred. When Saturday morning rolled around again they were reinvigorated, and this time they had a solid plan. They would take Vernon Johnson along. Vernon had been there before and would surely know the way to Camden Park.

Vernon said, "Sure, I know the way. All we have to do is, go to Prestonsburg, go north on 23, then east on Interstate 64, and it's on the left." Sounded easy enough, but they would take Vernon along just in case. The only problem was the fact that Vernon was only twelve years old. Two hours later they reached Interstate 64, drove east about ten miles, and there it was. The problem was how do you get into the place. There was no driveway. So, they drove past the park, turned in the median, and headed west. Again, no driveway, so they went through the median and to the east again. It had been more than a year since Vernon had been to Camden Park. But he said he remembered going down a ramp, turning left at the light, then left at the second light.

Vernon's directions worked, and they reached the park just before noon. The food and the entertainment were different from anything they had ever experienced. To say the least, it was a good time to be had by all. It was dark, and there was a long line of traffic when they were exiting the park. While they were stuck in traffic, Vernon fell asleep. He was exhausted and sleeping soundly when he heard low, soothing voices. "What a wonderful day," a woman's voice said. "And to top it all, we have this beautiful full moon rising directly in front of us."

In his subconscious state of mind, the meaning of the words didn't register right away. When he had fully processed the words, he realized the full moon should be coming up behind them, if they were on Interstate 64, or to their left if they were on US 23 headed south toward home. He suddenly snapped into the upright position, as they were passing a sign which read, Charleston West Virginia 8 miles. They had driven east on Interstate 64 for nearly seventy miles, instead of driving ten miles west, then south on 23.

Vernon got them headed in the right direction, and fell asleep again. This time however, the driver missed the exit for US 23, but they had only gone about twelve miles when Vernon instructed them to exit and turn east again. After that, Vernon didn't dare fall asleep again. They finally arrived home just before dawn, completely exhausted. However, there was never an ill word spoken about their wrong-way driving. They had enjoyed a day they would never forget. Agnes couldn't wait to tell all her friends. She told them about the food and the rides. Then she told them what intrigued her the most. She said, "We sure did drive past some pretty houses, and farms up there in Pennsylvania."

Chapter Five

Moonshine whiskey was a way of life, and enough folks drank it to keep the bootleggers in business. Some whiskey makers or dealers lived quite well. It was said that there were only two kinds of people who didn't dabble in the business in one form or another. Those two kinds were fools and liars. For this reason, a lot of folks kept secrets about their involvement with the stuff. There were, however, some young and boisterous men who made it no secret at all. They lived wild and free, on dangerous mountain roads. Tragically, this sometimes resulted in cold dead bodies being cut from the wreckage. Some were the wild and free, and some were innocent, unsuspecting victims. But for good, bad or evil, bootlegging and moonshine were there to stay.

Were moonshiners easy to recognize? you might ask. Not just by looking at them, but there were things that would give them away. The whole business was closely watched and policed by the Internal Revenue

Service. Why the IRS? Politicians would say it was to protect the good citizens from bad whiskey, and the evils of alcohol. Personally, I don't think the IRS gave two hoots about someone drinking bad liquor. The whole thing was because it was untaxed liquor. The Feds were not getting their share of the proceeds.

Bootleggers looked like everyone else. But if someone appeared to be a little better off financially than others, then that someone was looked upon with an eye of suspicion. Since everyone worked in the coal industry, everyone knew how much money each man was making. If you didn't have a job and you were still able to feed your family, you were accused of bootlegging. Our father was a suspect, and he didn't touch the stuff.

There was one bootlegger who did indeed look different. Her name was Lully Bates. Lully had a small farm on the other side of Abner Mountain, along the banks of Indian Creek. The house was a cottage with a Dutch-style roof with a couple of rooms upstairs. The outside was neatly painted white, with a full-length porch across the front of the house facing the road. The porch floor was painted battleship gray. The house, barn, outbuildings and fences were all painted white.

It was thought that Lully was a miner's widow who had been left with some savings, and perhaps a handsome life insurance policy. She was an older, but handsome lady. She had long light brown hair, medium height and very, um.... buxom. She cut and sold fresh flowers from her garden. When the flowers died she made wreaths from the stems. She also provided the same merchandise for Curt Tackett's general store, to be sold on consignment.

Lully also had some unusual and erratic behavior issues. You see, when the weather was warm she would sit outside in the nude. Or as southern folk would say, "Necked." That's right, as naked as the day of her birth. I had heard those rumors, but I didn't believe it. Therefore, my brother drove me past her place one morning just to prove it. Sure enough, there she was in all her glory.

After passing her place we drove on to Pikeville, where my brother had a couple of errands to run. On the way back he said, "Let's stop at Lully's place for a few cold ones."

I said, "You mean that crazy lady's place?"

He said, "She's not crazy. She's smarter than both you and I."

Lully was nowhere to be seen when we pulled into the driveway. We walked up onto the porch and knocked at the front door. When Lully opened the door, she was fully dressed complete with makeup. She spoke in a business-like tone when she asked, "Can I help you, gentlemen?"

My brother said, "We want twelve cold cans of Schlitz."

Lully looked at me suspiciously and said, "I know you, Jimmy, but who's your friend?"

Jimmy said, "This is my brother. He's got short hair because he is in the service."

She sold us the beer and we drove away, leaving me more confused than ever. Jimmy said, "She saw your haircut and thought you were a cop."

I said, "That lady has got all the makings of a crazy person."

Jimmy said, "Yeah, that's what everyone thinks. The cops, the people in the churches, everyone except her customers. As long as they think she's crazy, they won't mess with her." I heard all kinds of rumors about Lully, in the years to come. I heard she had a lot of money. One thing's for sure, she had a sure-fire way of covering up her bootlegging business.

Chapter Six

I've described Collier Rock in previous books, but in case you've never read those books I will describe it now. Collier Rock is a tall plateau located on a sharp ridge, in the south-east corner of Shop Hollow on a three-thousand-foot ridge. Having been to many places throughout the world, Collier Rock is among the prettiest places in my memory. From there one can see for thirty miles in every direction. It was hard to resist camping there on full moon nights when we were kids. Spring break, sultry summer nights, and autumn nights. It was a place of refuge even if the weather turned bad. There were safe, cozy shelters at the base of the cliff, and there was Lische cave nearby.

  We watched the most spectacular thunderstorms as lightning flashed above and sometimes on the slopes below. I remember one evening when a storm was coming in from the west. My brothers and I stood near the west edge of the cliff, watching as the storm moved closer. Suddenly on a slope far below, lightning struck a large tree. Every branch of that tree lit up as brightly as the lightning. The tree was close to a mile away, but even at that distance, the sound of the explosion was deafening. As lightning continued to flash, we could see that the tree had been blown to pieces, with smoke rising from its remains. There had not been a single drop of rain thus far, but we knew it was time to head for shelter.

I remember that hot and humid June of 1968, and how the world seemed to be locked into deep depression. Looking around, things appeared to be normal. The farm animals made their normal sounds and wallowed lazily in the summer heat. In the pastures the daisies grew, and the old folks talked of rain and cooler weather. But there was nothing normal about the world in the summer of 1968. We all wondered if the world was going crazy. The assassinations, the poor people's march on Washington, and the death toll in Vietnam averaged one hundred and thirty-five Americans per week, and countless Asians. Folks attempted to escape this in any way possible. My brothers and I found our escape on Collier Rock.

The main peak of that cliff pointed southward. Looking to the right from that peak, you could see a small but beautiful white cottage in a clearing deep in a hollow near the end of Long Fork Creek. I thought it must have been the house Massie Tackett was building as Lische watched from this point more than a hundred years before.

Looking to the left, Long Fork Road stretched to the east, where other houses were located along the south bank of Long Fork Creek. Those houses looked to be an equal distance from where I stood. Just a mile or two away, to my left and to my right. However, on the road, which wound its way along the creek, the distance was nearly ten miles from the house deep in the hollow to the houses to the east.

The world looked incredibly large from that lofty perch, but the large world looked to be at peace. The dark green mountains in the distance turned to a smoky blue just after sunset, and a whippoorwill, or the faint sound of a barking dog, were the only sounds to be heard. To the east, the sky grew darker as night approached. Soon after, a large yellow moon rose above the mountains. We felt as if we could remain there forever, but down there, and out there, was reality and like everyone else, we would have to face it.

For the most part, the people of the area were devoutly religious and wholesome. They worked hard and sent their children to school. Simple pleasures were cherished among the older folks. Summer, moonlight walks and barbeques. Horseshoes were pitched on full moon nights sometimes until dawn. We looked forward to the spring carnival at school, but the Halloween carnival was everyone's favorite, including the parents.

The school windows were decorated with witches, and cats made of black crate paper. Indian corn, small pumpkins and squash were displayed in windowsills.

Weeksbury had an eight-room schoolhouse. Students were taught first through eighth grade. After that, kids were bussed to high school at Wheelwright about five miles away. There were nearly five hundred of them at the beginning of the 1960s. I enrolled there the first day of September 1960. I was a shy little booger and when the teacher asked my name, I said Wynn. She asked me again, then wrote Win on the blackboard. This is how it was spelled until my parents caught on and corrected the teacher. I didn't know it then, but I would spend a lifetime repeating and spelling my name.

The years passed quickly and by the time I started the fourth grade, I realized something deeply disturbing. Some of my friends from the previous year didn't come back to school in the fall. It didn't take long for me to realize, people were moving away. Among them were Denice and Greg White. They were brother and sister, and those two were the nicest kids Charles and I had ever met. They were always smiling and friendly, and they never looked down on anyone. And then I was told they had moved to Knoxville.

I noticed other changes as well. There were less coal trucks, less men walking to work and there were fewer cars on the streets. I noticed homes with no curtains. There were untilled gardens and lawns that stood tall with weeds. Soon after that, stores and shops began to close.

When I had finished the eighth grade and ready to begin high school at Wheelwright, the number of children attending the Weeksbury school had dropped from five hundred to less than a hundred in eight years. The coal boom that had built the area had ended, and folks were leaving for jobs in the north. The auto assembly plants and steel mills of Ohio, Michigan and Indiana were booming. Anyone who wanted a job could have one. Even at ten years of age, I began to feel that I was being left behind. I just couldn't understand why my own family wasn't leaving.

But, those who stayed behind appeared to be doing well. Their children were well dressed. They brought wholesome lunches to school in trendy cartoon covered lunch boxes, or they had money to buy their meals at the lunchroom. I don't remember being envious of those children, but damn, we were poor. My father had been injured in a coal mine, and my mother didn't work, but I guess that's all I need to say on that subject.

We filled our lives with simple pleasures, and we didn't pay much attention to what others had or did. We saw the seasonal trends in what our classmates wore. Preppy little girls with their cute little Easter dresses, and Halloween costumes. And the boys flaunting their class rings, and their Varsity jackets. Our parents always managed to buy two new outfits for us when school started and brother that was it. Tear those up and you were on your own.

We celebrated good meals. We enjoyed the silly games we played and the adventures that were all around us. On Saturday nights my mother and elder sisters made special treats. Fruits and berries were canned in the summer, preserved for the winter. We had fresh eggs for meringue, it didn't take much more than that for delicious fruit pies. My sisters were always creative. They made home-made fudge, popcorn balls and the best French fries you ever tasted.

I remember our first Christmas tree. My brothers and I found a spruce tree on the other side of the mountain. We cut it down with a handsaw and took it home. My sisters, Linda and Marie, gathered nuts from a buckeye tree, and seed balls from a sycamore tree, and wrapped them in colored tin foil. They hung these multicolored balls from the tree and strung popcorn for garnish. I thought the tree was beautiful.

Down the road a mile or so was a row of houses. I remember the folks who lived in every house in that row. First there was Eddie Newsome, the Bates family, the Dutton family, Frank and Agnes Newsome, Lent and Martha Tackett, Patton Mullens, Darwin Vanover and Patton's son, Junior Mullins. Each one of those houses was decorated with electric Christmas lights. They were all nicely decorated, but the homes of Patton Mullins and his son Junior were always the prettiest.

The roofs of the house, the doors and windows were outlined with lights. They each had a large Santa, sleigh, and reindeer mounted on the porch tops. And I think it was Junior who had a life-size Santa, holding a Coca-Cola. The lights would flash on for a second, then off for a second. I remember how gloomy it was when the lights were taken down after the holidays.

It was as if the summer had drained our very souls. People appeared to be tired, their minds searching for a new will to accomplish. But then things would begin to change just before Halloween. The air was cool and fresh, but there was much more than that. There was a spirit that entered all of nature. A spirit that was good, but unexplainable. It was a spirit older than the wind. You could see it in the grouchiest old men, and the snobbiest of old women. People became more helpful, more energetic, and more wholesome. The spirit didn't choose, it was in everyone and it grew stronger as Christmas grew near. Folks called it the holiday spirit, but it was the spirit of Christmas.

When Christmas was over, spirits would grow tired once again through the long winter nights. But each day the days became a little brighter and a little longer, creating new and blissful energies. This time around it was called spring fever. There were renewed efforts and grandiose plans. New hopes, and new dreams that could only be doused by tragedy.

But death comes to everyone's door. And death is cold presents, capable of destroying the spirit of those closest to it. When death came to someone in Weeksbury, everyone mourned the loss. Those closest to the deceased wept. We felt the only way to share their burden was to weep as well. Hence, we did. We allowed their loss to become our own. We allowed their pain to become our pain, and their scars to fall on us as well. Death is a sad, and unpreventable occurrence, but it unites those around it like nothing else can. And Weeksbury was united in those days.

Our school principal was Inez Owens. We all knew her son Larry, and we remember when he was killed on his way to work, near Pikeville. That was the summer of 1966. The very next year one of our classmates was killed in a roll-over in Weeksbury. His name was James Preston Hall. Those two deaths were so powerful, and so emotional, that rich kids began to embrace the less fortunate kids.

Teachers were doing all they could to take our minds off the tragedies. They held a writing contest. We were allowed to select any subject, but we had to submit our stories within two weeks. I was beginning to think the only way I would be able to complete my story on time would be to copy some report from an encyclopedia. One day I had an epiphany. I was riding in a pickup truck with my cousin Joe. He stopped for gas and told the attendant to check the oil. The man poured a quart of oil into the engine, removed the can opener and tossed the can over a fence and onto the creek bank. That night I began writing an essay on soil conservation and wildlife. There was no refuse service in those days. Household garbage was burned, buried, or tossed in the creek. The garbage washed downstream to become someone else's problem. Appliances were taken to secluded mountain roads and tossed out. Coal was essential for America's prosperity. However, the search for coal, and the mining of it, was horrendous for the environment. It was a scathing report, but I wrote the truth as I knew it. My three-page report placed number one in the county, and gave me the first hint that I would someday be a writer.

When my uncle Jim Rice died, lots of people mourned our loss. But none more than Eddie B Newsome. The two of them had been friends since childhood. Uncle Jim passed away in August 1962. Eddie B Newsome died of an aneurysm on Easter weekend the next year. They were both far too young to die.

We lost community leaders as well. We lost two clergymen in the year 1963. Caine Blackburn, and Proc Middaugh. The Johnson Family Cemetery was close by, and it seemed that one funeral tent would be removed, only to be replaced by another. As humans, we've lost a lot of that unity along the way.

As the years have passed, mankind has become smarter and mankind has become dumber. Great and wondrous discoveries have been made, but mysteries and miracles have been lost. We witness many wondrous things in the course of a lifetime, and yet we only pray on our deathbeds. Mankind seems to be quick to denounce, and push away the goodness that is ready to enter each and every one of us. And without that goodness, what will become of our Earth?

There were so many things in the news in the 1960s it was hard to keep up with it all, but these are some things you might remember.

John F Kennedy defeated Richard Nixon to become the thirty-fifth president of the United States in November 1960. April 1961, Russian cosmonaut Yuri Gagarin became the first man in space. Less than a month later, Alan Shepard became the first American in space. Writer Ernest Hemingway died in July of the same year.

In February 1962, John Glenn piloted his Friendship 7 space module to become the first American to orbit the Earth. Actress Marilyn Monroe was found dead in August 1962. In October 1962 the world held its breath when Russian nuclear missiles were discovered on the island of Cuba. The entire US military was placed on high alert and a naval blockade surrounded the island. In an interview, years later former defense secretary Robert McNamara said that one wrong move during the crisis and eighty million Americans would have died. An equal number of Russians would have also died as well as everything that lived on the island of Cuba. Doctor Martin Luther King gave his famous "I have a dream" speech in Washington DC in August of 1963. President Kennedy was killed in November of that year. The news of the president's death took the focus from the search for a serial killer, who police were calling the Boston Strangler. The Beatles came to America just three months later, in February 1964.

In October 1964, The Saint Louis Cardinals defeated the New York Yankees in Game seven, of the World Series to become the World Champion. In November of 1964, Lyndon Johnson celebrated a landslide victory over Barry Goldwater in the presidential election.

Chapter Seven

At about the age of ten, I began helping my father and older brothers in the fields. We also cut large trees and produced timbers for the remaining coal mines. It wasn't all work and no play, however. We enjoyed every minute of our childhood.

As children, we noticed the ever-changing phases of the moon. There were no outdoor lights in Shop Hollow, so the night was only as bright as the moonlight or the starlight. We enjoyed playing outside in the moonlight, but we were careful not to wander beyond the perimeters of the yard. The danger of snakes was constant, mid-spring through late autumn. There were wild animals as well, and after the family dog became rabid and had to be killed, we were ever suspicious of all animals; wild or otherwise.

There was at least one old mountain lion that kept us mystified. We called it The Squallish. But like most cats, it had a natural dislike or fear of dogs, and our dad always kept hunting dogs. My brother Charles and I had our closest encounter with the big cat in the fall of 1967. We had been prospecting for ginseng. Ginseng is a rare and valuable herb, which we sold to R. T. Greer Herb Company of Pikeville. Finding the plant was and still is somewhat of a sport in that area, for those who know what to look for. We were several miles from home near the end of a hollow known as Crooked Branch. As the sun went out of sight behind a mountain we realized we had waited too long before heading for home.

We were not too concerned, we both knew the way, and there was a half-moon directly overhead for light. The shortest way back would have been the way we had come, which was back down the hollow then straight up and over the mountain. However, the light of the moon would soon be shadowed by the mountain, if we took that path. So, what we decided to do was continue up the mountain, as we were half way to the top already. We would then follow the ridgeline, back to the south and home in about four or five miles. This would take us in the opposite direction to home until we reached the ridgeline. It would also add some distance to our return. But we would have the light of the moon all the way if we stayed on the ridgeline. We would follow the ridge for about three miles then turn right and down the mountain to home.

We didn't realize that a forest fire had burned a few years before near the top of that mountain. The first things to regrow after a fire are wild grapevines, and locust trees. Locust trees have long, sharp thorns, coupled with grapevines making it nearly impossible to clear a path. We were both scratched, frustrated and covered with sweat when we finally reached the summit. We left at the ridgeline and onto an animal trail that led toward home. There was an old legend about a certain stretch of the path along the way. We would have to go through it or find a way around it. It was a strange and eerie stretch of about a quarter of a mile.

The strange thing about it is that no animal would travel that section of the path. The humblest dogs or horses would become vicious if you tried to force them to walk that trail. Old folks said the place was guarded by the spirits of a people who died perhaps a thousand years before white people came this region. We didn't have any clue as to the reason, but Charles and I had witnessed it on more than one occasion.

The most noticeable was when our sister Linda told everyone she could walk her dog Chico along that trail. Chico was a long-hair, black and white, humble old mutt. I swear that lazy old dog was as harmless as a rabbit. She tried leading him along with a leash, but he dropped to the ground. The dog growled, chewed at the leash, then he rolled as the leash wrapped around his neck to the point of choking him. Linda removed the leash from the collar and attempted to drag the dog with her hand through the collar. The dog became so vicious she had to release him. The entire incident took place in broad daylight.

The eerie part of the trail would have been a shortcut, and we would avoid crossing the tallest peak for miles around. The peak (known as the Old Knob) stretched high above the natural level of the ridgeline. The eerie trail was a footpath along the side of the peak and back onto the ridgeline. There were two trails which animals used to avoid the eerie trail. Animals would either go down the mountain a hundred yards or so, then turn and travel parallel to the path then back up the hill to the ridgeline on the other side. The other trail led up and over the Old Knob. There were trees on both sides of the eerie trail. The branches of those trees laced together to create a natural tunnel. That tunnel was dark and shaded even on the brightest of days. Imagine how dark it would have been at night with the moonlight shadowed by the mountain. There was no way we were going on that stretch of the trail.

We decided to take the trail which led up and over the peak, in order to remain in the moonlight. Near the summit we stopped to catch our breath. That's when we began to suspect that something was following us. It's hard to describe. We didn't hear any sounds, it was more of a feeling. When we reached the top, we stopped to listen. In the brush to our right, on the opposite side of the peak from the haunted path, we heard sounds in the leaves. We were sure that a ghost wouldn't make sounds in the leaves, so we were relieved to know it was an animal. We did, however, quicken our pace. Soon we started down the other side of the peak. Home was only a couple of miles away and it was downhill all the way. About halfway down the peak, we stopped to listen, and we heard the sound again. We didn't have a gun, but we both had strong throwing arms, so we hurled rocks in the direction of the sound. What we heard then was a low growl. We looked at each other and said, "Squallish."

With that we hurried on, looking carefully from side to side, but we didn't dare run. Running would have enticed the big cat to chase and attack. The mountain lion had only been seen a few times, and each time it had appeared to be shy, and elusive. The only things we had been taught about mountain lions were that they are powerful, swift, territorial and unpredictable. We were also told that humans were not on their menu, unless they were desperately hungry or provoked. We thought we might have wandered onto its territory or interrupted its hunt. For whatever the reason, we were terrified, and the animal seemed to know it.

The next time we heard it, the cat screamed. It had circled and was directly in front of us. It never crossed our minds that there could have been two cats. We left the trail and followed what had once been a wide path where cross-country phone lines had once been strung on poles. The poles and cables had been removed and the path was now overgrown waist-high with locust, blackberry, and grapevines. It would make the trip longer, but because it was downhill it was not as bad as what we had gone through earlier, in Crooked Branch. Anyway, this was the only way of avoiding the deep, dark shadows.

We couldn't have been more than a hundred yards from the pasture. Which meant that we were almost to the bottom of the mountain. The pasture had been cleared about two hundred yards up both sides of the mountain from the creek. The pasture was cleared to allow livestock to graze both sides of the mountain using the creek for water. Ours was the only house in Shop Hollow, and it was at the end of the hollow. The mountain lion had driven us almost to the entrance of the hollow, and quite a distance from home. From where we were we could see some lights of Weeksbury through the trees. We could also see two cows and two horses in the pasture down below. Suddenly the cows ran one direction and the horses ran another at full gallop. We knew the cat had cut us off and was again between us and home. We turned once again to the right, and down through the tall timber.

We finally reach the pasture, squeezed between the strands of barbed wire and into the pasture. We somehow knew the cat was toying with us. It could have attacked us at any time along the way. We followed the cow path which was still in the light of the moon. We only had about two hundred yards to go, and we'd be home. But the closer we got to home, the more frightened we became; and the harder it was to resist running. A hundred yards from the house we turned to see a quick glimpse of the cat, and it looked huge.

We jumped the creek and began to run, as we did the cat screamed once again, not far behind us. But the sound alerted the hunting dogs. They began to bark as they charged past us in pursuit of the big cat. We listened as the dogs chased the cat back through the pasture and into the tall timber. We were sure there would be a battle, but the cat was much too fast for the dogs. They stopped at the edge of the pasture where they stood in place, barked for some time, then came trotting home. Those faithful old dogs were our heroes, and we were always grateful, for they probably saved us that night.

We seldom ventured into the woods without the dogs after that, and it would be years before we told anyone about that night. As the years passed, we became more bold and fearless. We began to wonder what would have happened that night if we had faced our fears and confronted the cat. We are a family of animal lovers, but my brother Charles has hated cats since that night, more than fifty years ago.

Chapter Eight

My older brother Perry made a miniature log cabin and gave it to his fourth-grade teacher (Mrs Edna Frazier). He used grapevine for logs and wood chips for shingles. It was about four inches wide, twelve inches long and eight inches in height. Mrs Frazier treasured that little cabin. She placed it in the school window where class after class would have a chance to enjoy it.

My brother Charles and I were in the same class. We looked at the construction of that cabin and decided to try building the real thing. So, we asked our father for permission to cut the necessary trees for the construction, and he said yes. But we were only to use trees that were already dead. With nearly three hundred acres of dense forest, there were plenty of dead trees. We also included our younger brother Jimmy in the construction. He was only about eight years old, but he was bright and innovative.

September's bright sunny days made it almost unbearable to sit in a classroom when we had such a magnificent plan in mind. We rushed home and headed straight up the mountain in search of the right size trees. Sassafras was the perfect type of tree. Sassafras trees are not a large tree and they're a soft wood, lightweight and easy to handle. Within the first two hours, we had gathered four logs that were about eight inches across the base. The cabin would be eight feet wide and fourteen feet long. Another hour's work and we had the first set of logs in place. The logs were notched at the corners so that they fit closely together.

It was a slow process at first, but by the end of a full weekend we were ready to start the roof. Our father showed us how to split shingles from eighteen-inch sections of red-oak logs using a tool called a froe. We used the shingles to create a watertight roof. The space between the logs were chinked with mud and straw. We even built a fireplace using flat rocks and mud.

By mid-October the project was complete. We were proud of our cabin, and why not. It had a fireplace, a wood floor and windows with shutters. It didn't take much of a fire to make it warm and toasty inside. From the outside it looked like an authentic pioneer cabin. It stood about a hundred and fifty yards up the mountain, on a grassy slope almost like a piedmont, near the edge of the tall timber.

Kids came from all around to help ward off vicious Indian attacks and someone was designated sheriff to deal with outlaws. Sometimes grownups would come and join the fun. On chilly autumn evenings, we would make a fire in the fireplace and someone would tell what we called bear tales. They were not tales of bears, but any kind of a scary tale was considered a bear tale, or a tale of the moon.

We had two Uncle Jim's who were delightful storytellers. The first was our mother's only sibling. He was a humble, kind and soft-spoken person. He had a little dog he called Judy. That dog would sit on his lap for hours while Uncle Jim told stories. I don't know what happened to that little dog when Uncle Jim died. I like to think someone took it in and gave it a good home.

Uncle Jim Rice would tell stories until we began to fall asleep, then he would lead us to bed. But Uncle Jim didn't go to bed. He would sit in the next room in the dark and listen to Hank Williams records. I guess it's hard to sleep when you know you're dying. Cancer took him in August 1962, at the age of forty. It was sad to watch as he suffered long, before his death.

Then there was Uncle Jim Cisco. He came to the coal fields in the late 1930s, from somewhere in West Virginia. He met and married our father's sister Molly and they had six children. He was not a large fellow, but there was something commanding about him. He was always well dressed complete with a hat. There was not an ounce of fat on him and he spoke with a deep, voice. He was clean-cut and very intelligent. He didn't talk much, but when he did, he spoke with certainty. Jim was a wonderful father, who made sure his children received the best possible education.

Jim was a devoutly religious man who tried to convert those around him to a better way of life. He had two ways of doing this. The first was to convince you of the power and goodness of God. The other was to scare the daylights out of you with a promise of fire and brimstone for those who failed to convert.

There were as many children as the cabin would hold on a clear October evening. Uncle Jim was presiding over the gathering. First, we sang some religious songs and then he told stories. Jim didn't have to make up stories, for he had seen many, many incredible things in his life. You see, Jim was a hero in the First World War. Sure, he told stories of wicked beings. Stories of witches, demons and warlocks, just to entertain us. But he had witnessed the power of good, and the power of evil, first hand.

He told of how demons manifest themselves on the battlefield, to make men do unspeakable things. He told a story that stuck in my mind for the rest of my life. The event took place during the war, but it had taken place nearly four years before he went to war. However, it was a story that was still fresh in the minds of the soldiers who witnessed it.

It was August 1914, when a small British expeditionary force was surrounded and outnumbered four to one by the Germans just west of Mons Belgium. Just when the British were sure all was lost, a heavenly apparition of two angels appeared above the battlefield. One of the angels held a flaming sword, which led the English to believe it was the Angel Michael.

Then an army of bowmen joined the battle, fighting alongside the British soldiers, shooting clouds of arrows into the German ranks. German commanders were confused, and said they were unaware that the British had armies of archers. With the divine help, the British won the battle. The Germans couldn't understand how they could have lost with such an overwhelming force. After the battle, the Germans went onto the battlefield to collect their dead. They were even more confused to find countless dead Germans who had no apparent wounds. They made the claim that the British had used poison gas. However, they found no residue of poison gas on the dead soldiers. The incident became known as The Angels of Mons.

We enjoyed all the stories told by our elders, but that one was far more interesting. It was a Friday night and he had sent his own children home early to do their homework. He ended the evening with a short but scary story about witches and shapeshifters. We came out of the little cabin into the light of October's bright full moon. We paused for a moment before starting downhill toward home.

There were two paths leading down the hill. One went straight down to our house. The other went around the hill a short distance, then dropped down to the road leading out of the hollow. That is the path Uncle Jim took. The only light from home was the glow of the fireplace shining through the windows. The smell of burning hickory wood was a sweet and welcoming smell, and we would be home in just a few minutes. There were five of us, so we were not too afraid after the scary tales. As they say, "Safety in numbers." But looking up at the autumn moon it didn't take much imagination to see a wicked old witch fly past the moon, or to hear the howl of a werewolf.

For this reason, we were concerned about Uncle Jim. He was walking home alone, and his was a much longer walk. Not to mention the fact that there was the graveyard halfway down the hollow. Years later we would come to realize, Uncle Jim had seen the evils of war. There was nothing about the ghost of a dead friend, neighbor or loved-one that could frighten him. We watched him as he walked past the fodder shocks of the garden, down the hill then disappear from sight. It was a simpler time. A time when the only things people needed for entertainment were imagination and a good story.

Chapter Nine

By the time I was ten years old (1964), I was invited to join my older brothers when we were hired to work in gardens, mow weeds, clean barns etc. In May of 1966, we were hired to hoe corn for our cousin Joe. It was only about five acres located high on a hill overlooking a deep, green valley known as Indian Creek. The entire property consisted of ninety acres, and a house located on the south end of the valley. All of which was steep mountainside, most of it was covered with tall timber. However, there was an orchard of about twenty acres consisting of apple, peach, pear and cherry trees.

Back then, I wondered why Joe wanted five acres of corn. He only had one horse. Later I learned of his ulterior motive. Moonshine whiskey. He and our father were close in age and grew up together. They were almost like brothers, hence as children, we loved him as well.

The house stood on a cliff near the top of the mountain. There was a spring for water and a stream that flowed right next to the house. Electricity had never been installed to the house, and being there was like a step back in time. There was a covered porch along the north side of the house and along the west end. The porch on the west end was deeply shaded with apple tree branches. You could actually stand on the west end of that porch and pick golden delicious apples in late summer.

The porch along the north had a lofty view of the entire valley below. A few miles to the north you could see Indian mountain. Sometimes you could hear trucks laboring to climb the grade on the winding road. There were a couple of clearings where you could catch a glimpse of cars and trucks as they passed on that road. Standing there on that porch there were no worries. There were no appointments to run to, no cars to overheat or break down. It was a place of complete serenity. I described this property in a previous writing, so I hope the reader will be kind enough to forgive me if I'm being redundant.

There are two Joes in this story. The first was an old man who had helped my great, great grandfather plant the orchard and build the house more than sixty years before. The other Joe was his nephew. They were both related to me. The first was my grandfather's brother, therefore we called him Uncle Joe. The younger

Joe would have been my cousin. I will refer to them as Old Joe, and Young Joe. Old Joe had owned the house and orchard until about 1966 when the younger man convinced him to sell the property to him. From this point Old Joe will have little to do with the story, only his wife Liza. When I refer to Old Joe, I will also refer to Liza.

Joe didn't move into the old house when he bought it. He only used it for a hideaway when he wanted to escape his wife (Fanny) or other responsibilities. He had worked long and meticulously to fenagle his Uncle Joe out of the property. The uncle, whom we called Old Joe, and his wife Liza had moved when the land was sold. They now lived in a small shack at the bottom of the mountain along the west side of Indian Creek.

I guess the trip was about twenty miles from our house to what Young Joe was now calling his upper place. But the trip included about twelve miles of mountain driving. Crossing Abner Mountain, two miles along Indian Creek, and then straight up the mountain to the house. Joe would pick us up early in the morning, drop us off at the house on the rock, then return for us at the end of the day. Hoeing the corn took about two and a half days. We worked through the weekend, and then we would finish the field the following weekend. Then we would return to repeat the process in about three weeks.

Hoeing corn is a process for removing weeds and straightening the stalks. But this field was steep, and the soft black topsoil had washed away. What was left was rocks, milkweed, and wild grapevine roots. It was, to say the least, "challenging." However, it was such a beautiful place to work, and we were getting two dollars each per day.

I don't know if Joe paid his Aunt Liza to do it, but she made our lunch every day, but she called it dinner. It was about two hundred yards from the house to the field. And at twelve o'clock sharp, Liza would ring a triangular type dinner bell that could have been heard for miles. I still get hungry thinking about those meals. The food was cooked on a wood-burning stove. She made beef, or pork pot roast, with boiled potatoes, green beans, cornbread, and blackberry cobbler for dessert. There were no lights, so we ate in whatever the light of day provided through open doors or windows. Liza never joined us for the meals, and I don't remember hearing her speak. She would usually sit on the front porch swing while we were eating. We knew this because we would hear a quiet squeak in the porch swing chains. That sound, the chirping of the birds, and the ticking of a clock were the only sounds to be heard during the meal.

I like to think about Aunt Liza, that place, and the peacefulness of those times. I like to think about the youth and the innocence of those days. What I didn't know then was that the back-breaking labor was building a character within me that would follow me for the rest of my life. A character that would help me in days to come, when I would be tested to the very edge of human endurance.

I returned to that valley in the spring of 1968. Two of my elder brothers (Ernie and Dean), were working in a coal mine there for a man by the name of Lee Tackett. They had mentioned that Lee was in the market for some mining timbers. Mining timbers were cut from logs to the specific height of the coal mine tunnel. The required length for Lee's mine was 34 inches. Charles and I had spring break coming up and that would be a good opportunity to earn spending money. I was told that Lee would be at the mine site on Saturday until noon, along with a couple of the miners. However, my brothers would not be working that day. It was five miles or so on foot, through the mountains and down into that valley.

I set out early on a clear, frosty spring morning. The eastern face of the mountain was still shadowed from the sun, but when I reached the top it was a different day. The sun was bright and warm, the birds were singing, and the sky was blue. It was a perfect day. There's something totally invigorating about fresh air and mountain mornings. I began to hurry along, even though I was in no hurry.

In less than an hour, I was standing on the ridgeline looking down into that beautiful valley. In the distance to the north was Indian Mountain and its Abner Gap. Abner Gap is a low pass, and the only route between Floyd and Pike County for miles. It's important to note, the county line runs along the ridgeline. On the Floyd County side, the mountain is called Abner Mountain. On the Pike County side, the mountain is called Indian Mountain. Smoke was rising from chimneys in the few houses further down the valley along Indian Creek.

I'm not sure how long I stood there gazing at the splendor in the valley below, but I had to move on, for I had business down there. I walked down the steep grade, and paused again at the top of the field where my brothers and I had hoed corn. The ground was brown, with dead and broken cornstalks from the year before. But nature was waking throughout the valley. Buds were swelling on the trees, and some early spring flowers were coming up, but not yet blooming.

I walked down through the field and to the old house where Aunt Liza had cooked our meals. Again, I stopped to wonder how Joe and Liza could have given up this place. I looked around and the old house looked to be asleep, or dead. But I suppose winters had been harsh and secluded for the old couple here on the north slope of this mountain. However, on a day like that, it was nothing short of utopia. The orchard was beginning to blossom and perhaps a little early for this elevation as there could be another freeze.

I walked on down the hill, and over the bridge that crossed Indian Creek. On the left, silent and still, was the old shack that Joe and Liza now called home. Further down the road was Uncle Monk's place. His place looked to be nothing more than a poor and neglected shanty. Just then a vicious dog bolted from under Uncle Monk's porch and headed straight for me. I grabbed a rock and hurled it with almost deadly accuracy. The rock struck the foundation with a bang, and the dog stopped running, but he kept trying to sneak up behind me. But the dog could see that I had another rock in my hand, cocked and ready, so he kept his distance. Then I saw Uncle Monk closing the gate to a pasture where his mule Jim nibbled at a haystack.

The old man called to me, "Come on over and visit a spell."

I said, "I will on my way back, Uncle Monk."

Uncle Monk had been married to my grandfather's sister Dine until her death in 1964. I guess that old man just needed company. I walked about two hundred yards further to Lee Tackett's coal mine, and I was disappointed when I didn't see Lee's car at the site. There was one car parked at the site, which I recognized as belonging to Bart Lay of Weeksbury. I could see the mine and Bart's car from Monk's place. I decided to wait for Bart to come out of the mine and ask for a ride across the mountain to Weeksbury. In the meantime, I would walk back to Monk's place and visit until Bart came out of the mine.

I thought about Uncle Monk as I strolled back toward his house. He was quite a character. I don't believe he had ever been a coal miner, and at thirty-one he was beyond draft age when the US entered the First World War in 1918. Born in 1887, he spent most of his life plowing fields for other people. He had always used mules for farming, and for transportation. Mules are more suitable for the mountain terrain than a horse. They are simply more sure-footed than horses.

I was too young to understand what that old man was going through when his wife passed away. He was completely lost and alone. He would ride that mule from place to place in search of nothing more than conversation. Their only son, Charlie, left home shortly after her death to work in the coalfields of West Virginia. I had heard that Monk had taken a strong liking to the bottle after Dine's death. I can remember smelling liquor on him, but I personally had never seen him drunk.

My mother would make dinner after church on Sundays. That meal was served about mid-afternoon. Monk was never much of a church-goer, but he would often ride his mule, Old Jim, through the mountains and join us for Sunday dinner. After dinner, we would gather around him on the porch and he would tell stories. It had been a number of years since I had seen him, and doing the math in my head I figured him to be seventy-five years old.

He was in the front yard pruning branches from an apple tree when I approached the house. The dog came at me again, but without saying a word, Monk waved his hand and the dog cowered back into hiding. He met me with his hand out and asked, "So, whose boy, are you?" I told him, and he said, "My goodness, last time I seen you, you was just a little boy."

The old man wore coveralls, and the badly worn shoes on his feet had once been dress shoes. The hat he wore was worn to a shine and covered the little bit of white hair that remained on his head. His stubbled beard was white, and there was the stain of tobacco spittle in the corners of his mouth. Monk looked like a vagabond in every sense of the word, but I loved that old man dearly.

He said, "Help me get these folding chairs from the porch, and we'll sit out here in the sun." I told him of my intentions of catching a ride back across the mountain with one of the miners. He told me he had seen a car leave the mine an hour or so before. That didn't concern me, however, because the car that remained belonged to Bart Lay. What I didn't know was that Bart had a mechanical problem on the way to work. He had left his car behind and caught a ride with another miner.

Uncle Monk walked over to creekbank to spit out the tobacco he'd been chewing. He came back, sat down in one of the folding chairs, and asked about the family. He went on to say that he had not heard from anyone in a long time. He said he had gotten used to being alone. The only things he had in the world was that ugly old dog and that nineteen-year-old mule.

He started by telling me how he used to run the mountains just like me when he was young. He talked of a time before the coal mines, before the virgin timber was removed, and streams were rivers that flowed year-round. He told of seeing his cousin shot and killed in a gunfight, in the very hollow where I lived. He cleared his throat and said, "That was a long time ago." There was a long pause then he said, "Sixty-three years."

Then he talked about the young and happy days living with his wife and son on the mountaintop. He said, "Sure, we had some tough times, but we was young, and used to it. We was doin all right till the hailstorm come, took our crops and destroyed the fruit. That's when we moved here. Let's see, that was thirty-four years ago. See all them trees in that orchard? I can remember when your great-uncle Joe, and your great, great grandpappy, Lische, planted them trees."

It was getting late, and I was becoming concerned about getting a ride. I told him I'd better be going, but he said, "Wait a few minutes, and then we'll walk down to the mine together. Now, here's a strange story for you. It was about this time of the year, just after my wife died. I was havin a terrible time. I'd just stay in bed and sleep as much as I could. Then a friend from over at Shelbi Anna would bring me a bottle. I'd saddle up Old Jim, and we'd just ride the ridges till late at night. We was on a ridge a few miles east of here, just walkin along slowly. We was in no hurry to get home. It was like it is now. The buds were swelling, but weren't no leaves on the trees. There was no breeze, it was a quiet and peaceful night. A quarter moon had just gone below the horizon, and the stars looked like you could just reach right out and touch them. I wasn't thinkin bout anything particular, sept missin my wife.

"I first seen it comin out of the west. At first, I thought it was a bat, but it kept getting bigger, and I thought it was some kind of large bird. And then this feelin come over me. I pulled back on the reins and just stopped. That thing just kept getting bigger and bigger. Then it floated through the tree branches like they weren't even there. Then the stars began to disappear. And that thing settled down over Old Jim and me like a cold, wet blanket. I tell you, everything went completely black. I couldn't see anything, in any direction. I wanted to reach out to touch it, to try and understand what was happening, but I couldn't. Me and Old Jim, we were just frozen in place. And then that poor old mule started to shiver, I felt so sorry for him. And I finally yelled out, go on and take us if you're going to. I expected it to fly away with us, or leave us and fly away; one or the other. But pretty soon it began to fade, and the stars began to reappear.

"I knew I couldn't have walked. I stayed on Old Jim, but I could tell he didn't feel right. But, somehow, he got us home. I didn't want to leave him in the barn all alone, so I put that crazy dog out there with him. You know, that mule's never been the same. I never rode him after that. I just want him to live out his days in peace."

I hadn't said a word during the entire story. That old fellow had always told some delightful stories, but this one topped them all. And he was so poignant. Something happened to that old man up on that mountain. Perhaps nothing more than bad liquor, but something happened that was powerful enough to change him forever.

I got up and said, "That was quite a story, Uncle Monk. I'd better walk down to the mine and find out what's going on."

Monk got up and we walked down to the mine together, but when we got there, he said, "Fan's not running." I knew in an instant what he meant. You see, coal mines of that day consisted of two tunnels with entrances about a hundred yards apart. About two to three hundred yards in, the two tunnels would meet. At the entrance of one of the tunnels, a large high-speed electric fan was installed to circulate fresh air through the tunnels. The last man out of the mine would turn off the fan before going home. The fan wasn't running, and that meant there was no one inside the mine.

There was only one way I was going to get home, and that was to walk. What concerned me was that the sun had already gone down, and Monk had just told me one of the strangest tales of the moon I had ever heard. I tried not to let my concern show as Monk and I walked back to his house. He continued to talk, but as soon as we were directly in front of his house, I said, "Uncle Monk, I'd better be going, it'll be late when I get back." The old man stood waving and each time I looked back, he was still waving. And like so many people I've known, it never entered my mind that I would never see him again.

When I reached the top of the mountain, the evening was just as Monk had described in his story. A quarter moon was just about to sink below the mountains to the west. There was very little wind and the stars were bright. For about two miles the path was virtually level, until I reached the point where I would descend three thousand feet into Shop Hollow. However, within those two miles was the weird section of the trail, where animals feared to travel.

I took a short break to catch my breath. Then I hit that trail as fast as any human could run. There were so many thoughts going through my head, I didn't hear nor feel my feet pounding the path. Thoughts such as the number of years humans had walked these ridgelines, and the possibility of their spirits still here, and still watching over this eerie land. They had left behind an abundance of relics that could easily be found. Throughout our lives we've collected arrowheads, spearpoints, and occasionally an ax. No doubt these items were left by a stone-age people who predated Christopher Columbus.

Then I thought about the old mountain lion, and a cat's natural instinct to attack movement. I realized I would stand no chance of outrunning a mountain lion, but that didn't slow me down. I reached the point known as Spring Gap, where the trail led down into Shop Hollow and home. I didn't think about falling, I ran full speed right down the steep path. I had it in my mind that if something were to attack me, that something would have to stop a fast-moving and powerful momentum. I finally reached home without incident, but I would think about that night and that story for the rest of my life.

Chapter Ten

Christmas break began on or about the twenty-second day of December just before noon in 1968, and school would not start up again until after the first of the year. It was a beautiful day and Charles and I rushed home, then headed straight up the mountain in search of adventure. We frolicked along the ridgeline exploring every cliff and cave. We stopped on tall peaks to enjoy the scenery. It was unseasonably warm and dry, and so far, there had not been a cloud in the sky. Smoke from a brush fire rose above the mountain-tops far to the east, and the smell of wood smoke was pleasant in the air. School was OK but, this was freedom. To be young and to run free, never feeling pain, never tiring.

We got home well after sundown that evening, but we were not one bit tired. We were full of Christmas spirit, and excited about the long break from school. It had been a stressful year, but the last two weeks of it were going to be fun.

We attempted to watch an all-night horror movie marathon that weekend, but everyone was asleep by about one am. The excitement mounted as NASA launched Apollo 8 which would orbit the moon. Finally, we would know what was on the moon. The pictures began to appear on TV on Christmas Eve, but we were sadly disappointed. The astronauts orbited just sixty-nine miles above the surface of the moon. With powerful camera lenses the pictures clearly showed little or nothing there. Astronaut James Lovel read from the book of Genesis, and what I remember most was the line, Void and without light. He then wished everyone a Merry Christmas back on good Earth, then said goodnight.

There was no sign of green men or space monsters. This deflated most of our imagination, of space invaders. We found that most science fiction movies were just that, fiction. The year 1968 was coming to an end, and we were glad to see it go. The killing of Martin Luther King in April, and Robert Kennedy just two months later, was enough to sour the entire year. The world seemed to have gone crazy, and the worst was yet to come.

Richard Nixon was elected in 1968 and sworn into office as the nation's 37th president in January 1969. The war in Viet Nam reached its deadliest point in 1968 with The Tet offensive (the Chinese New Year). In the early morning hours of January 30th, every provincial capital in South Vietnam was attacked by the Viet Kong and North Vietnamese Army Regulars. There was heavy fighting throughout the country, and the large Marine base at Khe Sanh was under siege for seventy-five days. In every sense of the word, the year 1968 had been a disaster.

In July of 1969, Massachusetts Senator Ted Kennedy lost control of his car on Chappaquiddick Island Massachusetts, resulting in the drowning of Mary Jo Kopechne. Actress Sharon Tate and six others were murdered by the Charles Manson clan in August of 1969.

In July of that year, astronauts landed on the moon and confirmed there was little or nothing there. However, this did not change our fascination for the moon. The soft and silver splendor of the moon gave light to our world. We watched it from the time when the only thing to be seen was a sliver and a dark outline. This of course could be seen just above the western horizon shortly after sundown. A little more of the waxing moon would show the following day and it would be a little higher above the horizon. This of course continues until a large yellow moon rises in the east just after sundown. You know, it's funny, a lot of people live their entire lives and never notice it. But we lived our lives marveling at the splendor of the moon. And when the full moon began to wane, and to rise too late at night to stay up and enjoy it, we felt a sense of loss. It was almost as if a friend had gone away, until a couple of weeks had passed, and the new moon would return to light the world we knew.

The 1960s were without a doubt the most tumultuous decade in the history of our country, if not the world. Vietnam began as nothing more than a campaign, with a few military advisers. But in March 1965 things began to escalate when the first official combat troops were deployed. US Marines landed at Danang South Vietnam. It was a controversial war from the beginning. But it became even more so when the world learned of the My Lai Massacre. In March 1968, Lieutenant William Calley led his platoon into the village of My Lai on a search and destroy mission. The small village was about one hundred miles south-east of Da Nang. Calley ordered his men to open fire, and when it was over, nearly five hundred old men, women and children had been murdered. The massacre sparked widespread protests against an already unpopular war. Calley would face a general court-martial.

Before it ended in 1975, more than 58,000 Americans were killed or missing in Vietnam. The 1960s saw leaders murdered and cities burned in race and political riots. Let us not forget the six-day war in the Middle East.

A few wonderful things occurred as well. The Beatles came in 1964 and changed the sound of music. Other bands from England would follow in what disc jockeys called the British invasion. In sports, Sandy Koufax retired from baseball ending an eleven-year career beginning with the Brooklyn/Los Angeles Dodgers. It is said that Koufax was without a doubt the greatest pitcher to step onto the pitcher's mound. In January 1967, the Green Bay Packers defeated the Kansas City Chiefs at Memorial Coliseum in Los Angeles in what would become known as the Super Bowl. We watched the festivities at New York's Times Square at midnight on December 31st, 1969. Yeah, we watched the ball drop on TV to end the 1960s. A young Dick Clark was the host of the happy occasion. However, many of us said, "The 1960s, goodbye and good riddance."

Chapter Eleven

Life was not all fun and humor in Appalachia. From 1880 to 1940, five town marshals were killed in Weeksbury alone. The area was full of wonderful people. But like any city or community, we had some bad ones. There were tough, mountain men who had no fear of anything. The quiet ones were the most dangerous. Silence was often a way of safeguarding dark secrets. It was a place where murder was soon forgotten.

But there were other mysteries hidden deep in misty mountain hollows. There were legends and tales of the supernatural. Appalachia is vast and unpopulated. There are countless misty mountain hollows you can visit. Pick one and go there before dark. Make yourself comfortable and wait for dark. Turn off your light and be as quiet as possible. Then see what happens.

The area was settled for the most part by people of European descent. They brought with them many different skills and trades. And some of them brought with them some strange religious beliefs and practices. There was a commonly shared belief in a holy God above and a Devil somewhere below. They believed these two beings to be an undisputable fact. They believed that God could do anything, and the Devil roamed the earth among us at will.

The area was and is infested with snakes, and referring to the book of Genesis, the serpent was the Devil. After all, it was the serpent who convinced Eve to eat of the fruit of life. And any creature evil enough to oppose the will of God had to be the Devil in the eyes of some Appalachian churches.

Therefore, deadly vipers were sometimes used in church rituals. The rattlesnake was the snake of choice. The snake was held high and passed around by religious leaders. The snakes were teased and taunted. What better way of showing one's willingness to stand up to evil than to stand up to the Devil himself. Oddly enough, I, personally, have never heard of a member of one of those congregations being bitten by a snake during a ritual.

A church stood alone on a lonely hill in Weeksbury. There were no houses near the church. I believe it was a Baptist church at the time. You see, church denominations could change in those days by virtue of its leaders. Electric lights had been installed at the church, but they were not much brighter than the coal oil lamps had been. It was a time when churches were few in that area, therefore one church would serve an entire community. It was also a time when every word of the Bible was taken to heart. For instance, "Daniel spoke to the lion, and the lion spoke back."

According to the legend, it was just before Christmas during a rare Saturday evening gathering. Folks had come from miles around. The pews were filled and some of the men stood along the walls, for lack of seating. The pastor had stepped to the altar and was just about to begin. During a moment of complete silence, the closet door in the rear corner of the room creaked open. An image of a man appeared, and the entire congregation turned to face the closet. The image took one more step into the light revealing himself clearly to the crowd.

There were no sounds from the people. Not a sigh, a gasp, nor a moan. Only silence as they gazed in shock, frozen in terror. Within every detail of that image was everything biblical scholars had told them to look for in the Devil. The creature stood slowly looking over the crowd, without making a sound. Then stepped back into the closet. Suspecting an elaborate prank, the men rushed to the closet. They emptied the closet of everything it contained and found no sign of the mysterious visitor. They searched for secret doors or passages, but found none. To deepen the mystery, there was no attic space above the closet and no space beneath the floor.

This is a story that has been passed down to the children, and the children's children, of the people who were there that night. The men of the congregation were convinced, they had ruled out the possibility of a hoax. Could it have been mass hysteria? Or did the Devil visit that early twentieth-century congregation? To the people attending that little country church, it was as real as anything inside that building. The church is still standing, and if you would like to spend the night there some dark December night, I'm sure it could be arranged.

Chapter Twelve

There were tales and superstitions in Appalachia that were as old as the hills. I wrote about a haunted trail in previous pages. But there were tales of haunted houses as well. The first to come to mind was a house on a mountainside known as Mead Hill. It was a beautiful two-story home, neatly painted white, with a two-story wrap-around porch. There were two large chimneys indicating a cozy, opulent home. The house was built in the fashion of a southern plantation home. Although we had no plantations in southeast Kentucky. We had coal and timber.

The grounds were well kept, with a variety of fruit trees. Kentucky Highway 122 crossed Mead Hill through a low pass, or as we called it, a gap. The house stood about half way down the north slope of Mead Hill just off the road. It was one of the most beautiful estates in the area until the late 1960s. The first noticeable changes were in the summer of 1968 when the grounds were left unattended. The lawn became weeds, and un-gathered tree branches lay beneath the fruit trees. The next year the porches went un-swept, with wet, moldy leaves stuck to the floor. There were no longer lights shining from the windows and the paint began to peel. There was no question, this beautiful property had been vacated.

When you hear a bizarre rumor, you tend to ignore it. But when you hear the same rumor again and again and from lots of people, you begin to wonder if the story has credence. According to the rumor, a man and wife lived in the house with two small children. The man had been a long-time employee of Island Creek Coal Company of Price Kentucky just a few miles to the north on Route 122. But the man had another trade, a secret trade. He had a three-quarter ton pickup truck with overload springs for heavy hauling. He had signs on the truck indicating that he had a tree trimming and removal service.

What the truck was actually being used for was hauling moonshine whiskey. He was transporting the stuff in heavy metal containers that had been used for water containers by the military. The containers were placed in the back of the truck, then covered with fresh-cut wood. The average moonshine still would produce about eight to ten gallons per week, but this man had a larger plan. He visited multiple stills in Knott and Perry

Counties, delivering as much as forty gallons per week to whiskey sellers in Floyd County.

He was making an enormous amount of money. But he didn't have an unusual number of visitors to his home, or any of the symptoms that spelled bootlegger. Most bootleggers were afraid to make and transport moonshine. They were content to have someone else make and deliver the goods to them, and this man knew it. This put him in the position to control prices and how much was sold by the people he delivered to. If his customers didn't conform to his demands, they stood the chance of being tipped off to authorities.

All this was rumored to have been the motive that got him, and his family murdered. It is said that he had been expecting trouble. For that reason, he wanted to make sure the outside lights were working. One evening at dusk, he stepped out to replace the porch light bulb. The instant the light came on, he was shot down. His wife and two children were found in the back of the house near the back door. They were killed to keep them silent.

No one knows for sure, but one thing is undisputable. One of the most opulent homes in the area was abandoned. There was no living will, but a local bank held a small lien on the property, and no one came forward to pay the debt and claim the property. Next, came the rumors of hauntings. According to those rumors, the bank was willing to give the house to anyone who was willing to stay in it for three consecutive days and nights.

This much I know to be true. There was always a light burning on the front porch. But the rumor holds that the light continued to burn after the overhead power line had been removed by the power company. The house continued to fall into disrepair. But as long as it stood, there were tales of pale blue lights. Stories of silhouettes moving across the windows at night, and children crying.

I'm not sure if it continued to deteriorate, or fell victim to a forest fire. The last time I passed the property, the house was gone. The only things that remained were the two chimneys. In the early 2000s, a new road was built, bypassing the site of the house. But ask any local, and they will point you to the old Route 122 that crosses Mead Hill. If you are traveling south on old Highway 122, look for the two chimneys about half way up the mountain on the right.

Chapter Thirteen

There were tales of ritual practices that were not in any way connected to the church, or Christianity for that matter. There were those who believed they could achieve more prosperity in the practice of evil deeds. But it sometimes went beyond greed, cheating, and stealing. There were those who practiced what was referred to as the black arts, or more commonly known as heresy.

As we know, the word God is a shortened version of the word good, and the word Devil is a compilation of two words meaning the evil. Those who practiced the black arts denounced everything thought to be good, just as those who were devout denounced everything thought to be evil.

In February 1692, everyone in the small Massachusetts town of Salem was sure the Devil had come among them. It started when two adolescent girls were playing a game in front of a fireplace on a cold winter evening. They had a jar filled with broken glass. The superstition was that when an egg was broken and poured over the broken glass, it would settle to the bottom in the image of a future lover. But the experiment went wrong. The egg settled into the image of a coffin. The two girls immediately fell into incurable fits of hysteria.

The fits continued for days with no answers in sight until one day when the girls pointed their fingers at Bridget Bishop, saying that she had put a spell on them. Bishop was immediately tried and hanged for witchcraft. When it was over, nineteen people had been hanged, and one crushed to death. The most notable was the hanging of Sarah Good. Clergyman Nicolas Noyse followed Sarah Good to her execution trying to convince her to confess she was a witch. She looked down from the gallows and said, "You're a liar. I'm no more a witch than you are a wizard, and if you take my life away from me, God will give you blood to drink." Noyse developed a brain hemorrhage, and died bleeding from the mouth.

History has proven the innocence of those who were tried and executed in the Salem witch trials. However, the accusers, constables, the executioners, and the judge failed to look for the Devil within themselves.

I'll tell the story of an old and well-known hermit who lived a secluded life deep in a hollow in southeast

Kentucky. He died in 1949, but he has living relatives, for that reason I will not reveal his name. Through the first half of his life he attended church, taught school and was proud to be a good citizen. But when his wife died suddenly at a young age, he became angry. He was angry with everything, and everyone around him, and he was angry with God.

He ordered a book called *Malleus Maleficarum*, a Latin term for Hammer of Witches. The book was written in 1487, by Heinrich Kramer. The *Malleus Maleficarum* was a guidebook for obtaining confessions from witches. He had no interest in obtaining confessions, but he wanted to know all there was to know about sorcery. He studied other mysterious books with no titles, black bindings, and pages yellowed with age. He studied chants and rituals.

In many ancient religions, the sun was believed to be the face of God. The most common story I heard about his rituals was one called in Latin, Et tune ad Nobis. In English, The Turning Away. This was the final pledge to denounce God and accept Satan. He climbed to the mountaintop at dawn, where he waited for the sun to fully appear above the horizon. He cursed the sun, then turned his back and swore an allegiance to the Devil.

He used Satanic chants, prayers, and effigies to punish his enemies. He once said of his grandson (whom he despised), "That young bully won't be able to get out of bed in the morning." The next morning, the young bully, who was thirty years old and had never been sick a day in his life, was unable to get out of bed. He was carried from his home, placed on a horse-drawn sled and transported to the train then taken to the hospital in Martin. Screaming in pain and paralyzed from the waist down, he was immediately taken into surgery to remove a mysterious lump the size of a baseball. The lump was on his back, just above the belt-line and just under the skin. The surgeon was Doctor Samuel Circles. He said that in all the years of medical practice, he had never seen anything like it.

Chapter Fourteen

There were some strange practices within a certain church denomination as well. I will not mention the church by name nor the denomination. Judge not, lest ye be judged. Right? Well, I attended a couple of these churches when I was a kid, and it scared the living daylights out of me. If you've never heard anyone speak Glossolalia you might not understand. It is an ancient language thought to be the true language of God. The practice of speaking in tongues was revived early in the twentieth century by preachers Charles Parham and William Seymour. It was said to be the language used by Saint Paul the Apostle to speak directly to God. But even then, Paul was asked to refrain from using the language, and never without an interpreter.

I've seen ordinary, everyday people speak in tongues. They appear to go into a sort of trance, their eyes roll back, revealing nothing but white. Then the speaking begins. I saw other strange happenings as well.

You see, it is a common belief within those churches that if you are not a member of their congregation, then you are a sinner, bound for Hell. They believe sinners are sick with demons, and the sinner will have those demons until they have been exorcised.

These are not spiritual demons, but physical creatures said to resemble lizards without legs. I didn't see one of those creatures, but I saw a woman twist, writhe, and growl. Then she bent forward at the waist and appeared to vomit. A man stood in front of her with an open songbook to catch what she was regurgitating. He then held the songbook close to his chest, running from the church to rid the congregation of the evil.

There was a member of that church who had braces on her legs, a victim of polio. I saw her dance and rejoice as if her legs were completely healthy. I saw a woman hobble in who was grossly obese and struggling to walk. Ten minutes after she entered the building, she did a back-flip.

They are a people who believe they can make it rain on some crops and make others wilt in the dust. Could it be divine power? Could it be the effects of adrenalin? Could it be the power of suggestion? You may draw your own conclusions, or you may go and see for yourself. Was it Karl Marx who said, "Religion is the opiate of the masses"?

Chapter Fifteen

On a snowy Saturday morning in March 1970, I awoke to the sound of a vicious dog fight. I then heard my mother screaming for my father to hurry. Then I heard the ping of a breach loading shotgun as it was broken down into loading position. Before I could get to the window, I heard the K-pow of the shotgun, the yelp of a dog, then silence. Wild dogs had come down from the mountains and attacked my sister Linda's dog, Penny.

I heard my mother ask, "Is he dead?"

My father said, "No, but he's beat up pretty bad." The dog had been shaken by the alpha male of the pack, and all he could tell was that it was a large black dog that did most of the fighting. Penny had numerous puncture wounds, but if there was no internal bleeding he would probably recover. The dog was carried into the house and placed in the bathtub where Linda washed and treated its wounds with a penicillin ointment.

I guess I was as concerned about Linda as I was about the dog. Linda had worked for a while in Lexington. She spent one summer in Brick Town, New Jersey (a New York City suburb). Then she had a relationship with a man in Indiana, but that went sour and she came home broken hearted and defeated. She had the most tender heart, with the temper of a wildcat. Beyond everything else, Linda had always been an animal lover. She had nursed so many wild animals back to health. I remember an owl, a chipmunk, and a fox. No animal was turned away, even at the risk of rabies. She had been bitten, clawed and scratched, but that never stopped her from caring for animals. My father was still discussing the incident when my uncle Harold came in and asked what had happened.

Uncle Harold was an interesting fellow, who had found religion many years before. He was an all-right fellow, but he was sure that if something went wrong it was the work of the Devil. This incident was no different. He declared the large alpha male to be an apostate of Hell, and the other dogs were his demon followers. He also said the pack had attacked a pony that was owned by Enoch Hatfield just a couple of miles away. He said they would have killed the pony for sure, were they not driven away by shotgun fire. However, just as it had been that morning, the wild dogs were out of range of shotgun fire.

A late winter snow was falling that morning. There was about two inches of snow on the ground, and it seemed to be snowing harder by the minute. I told my parents I wanted to go after the dogs and kill them with a rifle and they said, "Absolutely not." I continued to insist, as Uncle Harold continued to talk of the danger the wild dogs were to the community. Harold admitted that he couldn't go after them. He didn't say why, but I knew why. The fact is he wore glasses that were thicker than the bottom of a pop bottle. I persisted through the morning and my parents never said yes, but they stopped saying no. I think they were sure that by now snow had covered the dog's trail, I would soon realize that and shut up about it.

I don't think anyone noticed when I left the room. I dressed as warmly as I could, even though it didn't seem to be cold at all. I slipped out the back door with a .30-30 Winchester rifle and nine rounds of ammunition. Now that I was outside I felt an urgency to pick up the trail of the dogs, if I could even find it. Large snowflakes were falling so heavy and wet, as if it could change to rain at any minute.

I reached the site where the attack had taken place, which was about two hundred yards from the house. Kicking around in the snow, I found bloodstain. However, it might have been the blood of our dog; although my father thought a few buck-shot had hit the black dog. The falling snow had not completely hidden the dog's tracks. So off I went following the tracks along the stream toward the head of the hollow. Another two hundred yards, and the stream split. One stream flowed in from the right and the other flowed from straight up the mountain. The dogs had followed the stream that led upward, but the snow was quickly covering their tracks.

I was trying to stay focused on the trail, but I knew I would soon lose it. I began to think I would never see those dogs. My mind began to wander, and I was beginning to realize this would be another failure. I was about to give up, but is that how I would allow my life to be? Was I always going to allow failure to be an option? I had thought myself tougher than that, so I pushed onward through the snow. Everyone knew it was snowing. I could turn back now, and simply say, "Lost their trail in the snow." And no one would question me. But not this time, I wasn't through yet.

Wild dogs are not indigenous to the Kentucky mountains, they are created by irresponsible people. Unwanted dogs were taken to uninhabited places along the road and simply abandoned. The dogs are left to live and breed in the wild. Most of them are mongrel mutts but they are wild animals. People in those days ridded themselves of their household garbage as well. Abner Mountain, Jacks Creek, and Buckingham Mountains are examples of this. It is also a breeding ground and a feeding ground for wild dogs.

I came to a large oak tree branch that had blown from a tree the summer before. The leaves were brown, but they had remained on the branch. The dogs had hidden in this branch to rest and to shelter. This led me to believe that one or more of them was injured. For whatever the reason, it was a lucky break for me. The tracks leading from the brush were fresher and easier to follow. It must have been about noon by then, and the snow continued to fall. There was about six inches on the ground by then.

There are places in the eastern mountains that are extremely steep and difficult to climb. Having snow on the ground made it even tougher, and I was beginning to sweat. Just then I heard the "burff" sound of a dog. The kind of sound a dog makes when he almost barks, but didn't really mean to. I looked up and there on a cliff about sixty yards and off to my right was a large, black dog. It had to be the alpha male. I raised the rifle to my shoulder, took aim with my right forefinger on the trigger. I was thinking to myself that this was going to be a lot easier than I had thought.

Suddenly there was a loud thunderous roar that startled me. It was a fighter jet that had made the roar. The mountain terrain in that area was somewhat like the terrain in Vietnam. Military pilots practiced strafing runs over the area. I only took my eyes from the target for a split second, and the dog was gone. My heart sank, for I was sure I wouldn't get another chance for a shot like that one. I lowered the rifle, turned and took a long look back down the steep and rugged mountain. I was thinking how I was wasting my Saturday and how I should forget this foolishness and go home. But I didn't do that, I thought about Linda's dog, I turned and pushed onward.

I was finding it hard to stay focused. It was as if climbing this mountain was taking all my concentration. I had not been paying attention when the dog barked. If I had been, this chase might have ended here and now. I began to question my purpose for being on this hunt. Sure, I wanted to avenge Linda's dog, to kill that menacing pack of wild animals. But, were there other reasons? Was I trying to prove something to someone, or trying to be a hero. I was no hero. I wouldn't be sixteen until June. Again, I just didn't want to start my adult life giving myself the option of quitting.

Snow was beginning to erase the trail again when I finally reached the top of the mountain. And to my dismay, the pack had headed straight down the other side. This was extremely disheartening. I had hoped they would travel the ridgeline long enough for me to get close enough for another shot. I was determined not to be a quitter. I headed straight down that mountain, following what was left of the trail.

Spring would come in just over two weeks, but looking out at those snowy mountains it looked as if spring would never come. Going downhill was much easier but snow packs were pushing up under the legs of my trousers, freezing and chafing my legs. About half way down the mountain I found another place at the bottom of a cliff where the dogs had rested. Once again, beyond that spot the tracks were fresh and easier to follow.

Near the bottom of the mountain there was a gentle rolling slope and a clearing. About a quarter of a mile further down the hollow was a small house and various outbuildings. I could hear the cackle of chickens and I knew the dogs were raiding a henhouse. I heard the crack of a gun and saw the dogs running up the mountain in a sharp left turn to the north. I rushed around the side of the mountain in an effort to cut them off. My guess is that whoever fired the shot had missed; I saw five dogs running and I don't believe there had ever been more than that.

When I got to the spot where I was sure I would intercept the pack, I found nothing. The only thing I could do was go back down again in the direction of the farmhouse and see if I could pick up their trail. Until now the dogs had traveled in a straight line to the southeast. They only turned north after being shot at. About two hundred yards from the farmhouse I found their tracks along with some blood and feathers. Once again, they had turned and were headed straight due east. My hope was that they would stop to feast on their stolen chickens. I had no watch but looking up at the sky

I could tell it was getting late. I turned to look back at the steep tower of a mountain I had just crossed. Crossing it at night through the snow would be extremely difficult and I was already tired. But I was sure the dogs would stop to rest and eat. If I rushed ahead, I could probably catch up with them, and that would be the only chance I would need.

Wild dogs usually roam and wander in no particular direction. These dogs seemed to know exactly where they were going. Another hour and I was on a hill overlooking the small village of Virgie. It would be a gamble, but I decided to go down to the road and follow it to the east. I could move much faster on the road and perhaps get ahead of the dogs and cut them off. To get to the road I would have to cross Long Fork Creek. My feet were already wet, but I was not going to wade through that icy water. I walked along the creek bank until I came to a narrow footbridge that led to an abandoned shack. I crossed the creek and onto Long Fork Road. The snow had slowed to flurries for a while, but then it began to fall even faster than before, and it was getting dark.

The road had not yet been plowed, and there were only trails on either side of the road from the few cars that had passed. Each time one approached, I had to step off the road and into the deep snow until it passed. Funny, they all seemed to be going in the opposite direction. I was going east and everyone else was headed west. But I guess it didn't matter, no one would offer a lift to someone carrying a gun on such a miserable night. Somewhere above the snow and the clouds was an almost full moon, which made the night a little brighter. My eyes would adjust to the night, only to be temporarily blinded by the headlights of another approaching car. Up ahead on the left I could see the dim glow of a green and red sign. As I got closer, I could see that it was an electric Seven Up sign, in front of a small gas station.

I rushed toward the little station, with the hope of getting warm for the first time since I left home. Then it occurred to me that I left before breakfast, and had not eaten a bite since yesterday. A bell jingled as I walked through the front door. It was a small place with one light bulb hanging near the center of the room and a wood-burning stove beneath it. A man suddenly jumped up behind the counter with a frightened look on his face, with his hands out in front of him. I realized he was frightened by the gun I was carrying, and I was startled as well. "Hold it, sir," I said to him. "I just wanted to warm myself by your heater."

He said, "That's a good way to get yourself shot, packing a gun into a man's establishment. Anyway, you're just a kid. What on earth are you doing wandering around on a night like this, and where are you going?"

I explained about the dogs and asked if I could stand by the heater. I told him I lived in Weeksbury, and that I had tracked the dogs since mid-morning. He said, "Why sure, I'll throw in some more firewood." I asked if he had seen any stray dogs that might be part of the pack, and he said, "No, I've heard about them, but nothing since last fall. I heard they were attacking everything in their path. Cats, dogs, chickens, sheep, you name it. Old man Paul Kasten ran across them when he was rabbit hunting back in November. He said they would have had him, for sure, if he hadn't blasted them with his shotgun. In fact, he claimed to have killed one of them, but no one believed him."

"Why wouldn't anyone believe him?"

"Because he and Tommy Collins went back the next day to bury the dog and it was gone. He swore to Tommy that he shot that dog at close range with a twelve-gauge shotgun. He said that after he shot it, he punched it with the barrel of the gun, and the dog didn't move. He also said it was a bloody mess. But when he and Tommy went back to that spot, there was no dog, and no bloody mess."

I said, "Well maybe they went to the wrong spot."

He said, "No, not that old man. Old Paul knows his way around these hills. What did you say your name was?"

"Well, sir, I didn't, but my name is Wynn."

He said, "I'm sorry. What is your name?" I repeated my name and he shook his head and said, "Well, it's a different kind of name, I'll tell you that. My name is Don Hall."

He said, "You're welcome to stay here for the night if you like. I sleep upstairs, but I don't have an extra bed. You can stretch out here on the floor if you like. I don't have much for food. I can offer you a Milky Way, a bag of chips and a Pepsi."

I said, "No, that's OK. I don't have any money."

He said, "It's only thirty-five cents. Don't worry about it. Someday you'll have an opportunity to help someone and you'll remember this night." As I ate the food, I could feel a new energy growing within me; and a realization that the big cruel world had a lot of wonderful people on it.

I thanked him for everything, but I said I would like to stay just long enough to finish drying my hat and my gloves; then I would be on my way. He said, "You're not going to continue chasing those dogs, are you?"

I told him if I didn't catch up with them now, then I probably never would. I also told him that at this point, it would be just as easy to continue east along the road and cross the mountain at Abner Gap. "If I'm lucky someone will come along who knows me and give me a ride."

He said his parents had owned the station, but they died and left it to him. He said, "You know, my parents made a good living with this place. That's when there were coal mines everywhere. Folks had money back then, right up to the mid-fifties. I get by, but that's about it. I keep hoping the good old days will come back, but there's not much chance in that."

The little store contained a fine collection of junk. There were stacks of sports magazines on the shelves. The walls were covered with calendars, and license plates from years gone by. The counter was glass and contained stacks of baseball cards. There was only one gas pump outside, with only one grade of gasoline. The building was built of cinder blocks and looked to be straight out of the 1930s. The floor was concrete, worn slick from many years of footsteps. I hope I was able to describe that little station clearly to the reader, for it's a memory that I do not want to forget.

The night felt much colder when I left the little station. I walked out to the road and continued walking east, in the trails that were left by passing cars. I swear to you I hadn't walked more than a couple of hundred yards when the dogs came up from the creek and crossed the road just ahead of me. It was almost as if they had been waiting for me. I slammed the gun to my shoulder and took aim, but they were aligned with a house and I was afraid that a stray bullet would hit the house. I would have to wait for another opportunity, but the dogs ran up the mountain and disappeared into a pine grove. I ran after them as fast as I could go. I wanted to end this here and now, close to the road, then try and hitch a ride home. I got to the pine grove, and the dogs were gone, but their tracks were fresh once again and easy to follow.

The snow had stopped falling, and the moon was shining through thin clouds. The night was bright enough to follow the trail, but the moon would sink behind the horizon within a couple of hours, and the night would become much darker. But, with any luck at all, I would have this matter settled by then. I took a deep breath, and with a fresh shot of adrenalin, I started climbing yet another mountain.

I was sure I caught a glimpse of the black dog not far in front of me, and without thinking I drew the rifle into position and fired. I thought about what a foolish thing I had just done. I fired without knowing for sure, and that shot in the dark would only cause the dogs to run. It was getting late when I reached the top of the mountain. The moon was almost gone, and there was a steady wind blowing from the east. It wasn't really a cave, but there was a space at the base of a cliff that had been sheltered from the snow. It was on the west side of the mountain, just below the summit. I was sheltered from the wind there, and the moon was still giving light. I decided to make a fire, warm my feet and rest for a while.

I had everything I needed to start a fire. It's something I learned from my father. I learned to carry a few sheets of paper and matches in a waterproof container. The container happened to be a metal Prince Albert tobacco can. I gathered dry leaves, pine needles, and what I thought would be enough firewood. I made a small fire as close the face of the cliff as possible and let it burn for about half an hour while I gathered more firewood. I then took a long stick and pulled the fire away from the face of the rock. This would give a warm place to sit, and a warm rock to lean on.

With a warm fire in front of me, the warm rock behind me, and a loaded rifle across my lap, I soon fell asleep. I guess I hadn't realized just how tired I was or how long I had been asleep; but I was awakened by the mournful, chilling sound of a dog's howl. The moon had sunk behind the mountains to the west, and the fire was nothing but embers. It was a cold, dark and silent night. There's nothing more unnerving than complete, eerie silence. I scrambled to relight the fire, and it didn't take long, but it was too late, I was already chilled to the bone. The rock behind me had gone cold, indeed, the night had gone cold.

I was too cold and miserable to go on, I would have to wait until dawn. The fire felt good, but I needed to warm my backside. But, somewhere out there was a pack of wild and dangerous animals. There's no way I was going to turn my back to the fire. I would keep my back to that cliff and the rifle at the ready. There was that chilling howl again. Funny thing about snow, it muffles echoes and makes it difficult to know what direction sounds are coming from.

I had begun to shake uncontrollably as the night dragged on. I was making every effort to stay awake and alert, but I was exhausted. I needed to rest. Tomorrow would be another long day. But the short naps only brought terrible dreams. Visions of wolves, tearing at my neck and limbs. Dreams of glowing red eyes watching from the brush, waiting for a chance to pounce. This gave me time to wonder if Uncle Harold had been right. *Were these dogs' demons, or something even more evil than just wild animals, trying to survive? And then there was the story the Kasten man had told. The story that he had killed one of them, only to have it disappear without a trace.*

The firewood was gone, and I felt like jumping for joy when I saw that the stars had faded, and the sky was gray with the dawn. I got to my feet and looked around to determine what direction I should go. I was shocked when I saw dog tracks within fifteen feet of my campsite. They had visited me during the night, and now I realized that some of the nightmares had been real.

Fear had subsided and was replaced by anger, and a stronger determination than I had ever felt. The tracks led straight up and over the summit, straight down the other side, and continued to the east. I was moving as fast as I could go down that mountain. Running, jumping, falling, rolling.

Near the bottom, I heard the cackle of chickens again as another henhouse was being raided. There was a small house, a barn and pasture. The chickens were apparently being kept in the barn. Suddenly, the dogs ran from the back of the barn and up the mountain. It was going to be a long shot, but I was going to take it. The large black dog was leading the pack. I aimed the rifle slightly in front of the dog to allow for distance. Before I could pull the trigger, the dog leaped straight up into the air, as high as a dog could jump, then crumpled to the ground. Then I heard the report of a rifle, and saw a man running toward the pack. He stopped and fired again, and I saw a puff of snow behind the dogs and I knew the second shot had missed. I fired a shot as well, but the dogs had already gone out of sight into the brush.

I saw the man walking with a limp as he approached the dog that he had just shot, so I ran to meet him. When he saw me, he yelled, "This your dog, kid?"

I was tired and out of breath, the only thing I could say was, "No."

He said, "Well, they just raided my barn, and it's not the first time."

I finally managed to tell him that I had been tracking them since the morning before. Then I asked, "Are you sure that one's dead?"

He answered, "Oh, he's dead all right. I got him square through the neck."

He said, "Kid, you look like death warmed over. Did you sleep in the woods last night?"

I said, "Yes, at the base of a small cliff, just on the other side of that mountain. At least, I tried to sleep."

He said, "What's your name, and where are you from?"

I said, "My name is Wynn, and I live in Weeksbury."

He said, "Weeksbury? That's over in Floyd County isn't it?"

I said, "Yeah, I live near the border of Floyd and Pike County."

He said, "My name is Tim Calder. My wife and I have this little five-acre farm here, and that's all we've got. It's no fun when someone else's dogs come along to take away the little that we have."

I said, "I don't think these dogs belong to anyone. They're just dangerous, wild animals. They were tearing my sister's dog apart. They'll attack anything."

He poked the dead dog in the side and said, "This one won't be attacking anything."

"Are you ready to give it up now?" he said.

"No, now that you've killed the leader, I think I can catch up with them and finish the job."

He said, "I would go with you, but I broke my ankle last summer and I'm still having trouble getting around." He then said, "Well, son, don't spend another night in the wilderness. I think you've been lucky so far."

We said our goodbyes and I set out again following the tracks eastward. At this rate, I would be in Pound Virginia by nightfall. I was becoming complacent again when suddenly I saw a shaggy black and white dog standing on a log about one hundred yards away. I was careful not to move too quickly. I moved the rifle slowly to my shoulder, aimed, and fired. The dog dropped out of sight behind the log. I rushed to the log and there was the lifeless body of the dog on the ground. I breathed a sigh of relief, and thought, *only three to go.*

Success had invigorated me, and I hurried to catch up with the rest of the pack. I kept thinking that these dogs knew where they were going. The angle of the sun made me realize it was late afternoon. I was just about to turn back when the trail led into a deep hollow, and what looked to be a deserted farmhouse. I followed the trail, but I was ready to give it up. If the trail led beyond that house, I would not follow. I could see the dogs now, they were not running, but they were moving directly toward that old house. I moved to within a hundred yards of the house and hid myself in a gully.

The sun was shining, but this was a dark and eerie place. It was one of those places where the shadow of the mountains was almost constant. The place looked to have been deserted for years. One can imagine that most old deserted houses were once happy and prosperous homes. But not this one. I don't believe there was ever a happy moment at this place. The two-story house had a missing window pane in one of the two windows facing the front of the house.

There was a well, but there were no tracks leading to it. There were outbuildings, but no sign of livestock. There were two chimneys, but no smoke rising from them. There were fenced areas, including the front yard, but nothing in them but tall, dead weeds. Two large maple trees stood in front of the house that blocked most of my view. I moved to a better vantage point where I could see the entire house.

A creek flowed in front of the house, and what looked to be a wagon trail that led past the house and into a dense forest. A small footbridge led from the wagon trail, crossing the creek with a gate for entering the yard. What I noticed next was even more unnerving. There were images of animals made of sticks and straw. There were birds, dogs, horses, cows and humans. The images were hung from the maple trees, and most of them had stakes driven through them. Children could never be so diabolical as to make such vile images. It might have been my imagination, but I believed those things were effigies that were used in some sort of ritual. I just wanted to get away from that place. There was an indescribable sense of evil there.

That's when I realized there were no tracks leading to the house, and no other sign that anyone was living there. I felt relieved. I was now more than willing to give it up, find a road, and hitch a ride home. That's when the front door of the old house slowly opened, and an old couple stepped out onto the porch. They were just an elderly couple, but there was something odd about them. They both had silver hair. Neither of them wore a hat nor spectacles. The woman wore a long dark brown dress and ankle-high boots. The man wore dark-colored clothing as well. They looked like a couple from an old west TV show.

The woman remained on the porch and the man walked slowly toward the gate. The dogs were coming up the trail. They were in no hurry, nor did the man hurry to the gate, but man and dogs reached the gate at the same time. The old man unlatched the gate and allowed the dogs to enter the yard. He did not greet the dogs, nor did the dogs greet him. They stood by the old man as he looked slowly all around. It was as if he was looking to see if he was being watched, or perhaps looking for the other two dogs. He did not speak to the dogs, and the dogs didn't as much as wag a tail. The dogs simply followed as the old man walked slowly back toward the open door. I won't say he floated across the yard, but I've never seen a person walk so smoothly. I would not have thought him to be real, if not for the tracks he left in the snow. He and the dogs reached the front porch, and again there were no words spoken. The old couple and the dogs entered the house and closed the door.

I made no effort to stay out of sight when I left that place. I had a loaded rifle and I would shoot anything that posed a threat to me. I strolled right out on to that wagon trail and followed it along the creek. I knew that trail or that creek would eventually lead to civilization, or at least a road where I could hitch a ride.

It must have taken two hours of fast walking, but I came to a well-traveled two-lane highway. I walked along that road for about a mile when an old blue pickup truck pulled over in front of me. A man yelled, "Come on, I'll give you a lift." When I got to the passenger's side, I realized it was Tim Calder. He said, "Hop in, I've been looking for you."

I told him everything that had happened, the old couple, the dogs, the old house, and the effigies. He said, "Yeah, there's all kinds of tales and legends about that place. No one around here will go near it. I'm sorry, there's not much of a heater in this thing. Which way do you want to go?"

I said, "North, I guess, toward Abner Mountain."

He said, "We'll have to go south a little way, then we'll pick up US 23, then turn north. I'll take you as far as Indian Creek Junction. There's a grocery store there, you shouldn't have any trouble getting a ride from there."

I then asked him, "So, Tim, did you go back and bury that dog?"

He said, "No, but I plan to. Why do you ask?"

I said, "Well, I just wonder if it's still there."

He said, "You're giving me the creeps."

I said, "Yeah, I'm sorry, I guess I don't really want to know if it's there or not. I've had enough."

It seemed like weeks since I left home. I tried hard not to, but I fell asleep almost instantly. The next thing I knew, Tim was tapping me on the left shoulder. He said, "Sorry, son, this is as far as I can take you." I expressed my appreciation as best I could, shook hands with Tim and said goodbye.

I walked around to the front of the building, and I couldn't believe my eyes. There was my cousin Joe, pumping gas into his pickup truck. I approached him, and he said, "Wynn, where on earth did you come from, and what are you doing with that gun?" Joe and his wife Fanny lived on the other side of Abner Mountain, and hopefully he was on his way home. I told him a shortened version of the story and asked if he would be going home soon. He said, "Yeah, as soon as I visit Lully, I will be."

The truck was warm and comfortable. I said to him, "Joe, if anyone asked would you tell them I stayed overnight at your place last night?"

I fell asleep again and the next thing I knew I was home. Joe knew I was too tired to walk, so he drove me all the way home. He also knew I was in for some loud scolding, and he didn't stick around for it. He just said, "I'll see you later." And drove away. I got scolded and lectured, but I knew I deserved every word of it.

Chapter Sixteen

Like everyone my age, I wanted to be a Beatle. The fourth of July celebration was held at the Weeksbury Community Center, on Saturday July fourth, 1970. Our little band had been invited to play our four-song repertoire at that event. There was no stage, just a concrete platform with basketball hoops on either end. It was a bright sunny day, and a little cooler than normal for that time of year.

Surrounding the concrete platform was about an acre of land that had been mowed for other activities. Everyone who was someone was there that day, and the air was filled with the smell of roasting hotdogs and freshly mowed grass clippings drying in the summer sun. There were people from as far as twenty miles away. Many of them I knew, and many of them I did not.

Our band had a captive audience, although looking back I'm sure it was not much more than a racket. When we had finished, and it was obvious we wouldn't be playing any more, the people began to wander away to other amusements. We went about the business of unplugging amps, rolling up cables, and packing away instruments. We were almost done with our task when a soft voice spoke from behind me, "Wynn?" I turned around and there was this beautiful young lady looking at me inquisitively. "Wynn, is it you?"

I matched the sweet voice with the sweet face, then added seven years. I then realized she was Denice White. I was a shy backwoods boy. I had no idea what to say to her. We made small-talk, and then I asked, "Where's Greg?"

She said, "Oh, he's around here somewhere. The last time I saw him he was inside the community center playing a pinball machine. Where's Charles?"

I told her I wasn't sure where Charles was at the moment, but I knew he would be excited to see the two of them. Then I said, "So, I heard you moved to Knoxville."

She said, "Yes, we had just finished third grade. Remember?"

I said, "Well, Charles and I weren't sure what had happened to you, but when you didn't come back to school that fall, we knew you were gone for good. So, what brings you back, and please tell me it's permanent."

She said, "No, I'm afraid it's only for a couple of weeks. We came back to visit my grandparents. Do you know Kline Hall?"

I said, "No, I know of him."

She said, "Well, do you see that house with the large poplar tree in the yard?"

I was looking with great interest at the row of houses, across the train tracks, across the creek, across the road, and about a quarter of a mile down the road. "The one with the green roof?"

She said, "No, the one with the white car in the driveway. That's Grandpa's house, and that's my dad's car."

She said, "Well, I don't want to keep you from what you were doing."

One of the guys from the band (I think it was Junior Woods), spoke up and said, "Hey, Wynn, we can handle this. Go on and do your thing."

We started walking along the railroad, without even noticing that we were walking. We talked about everything, and we talked about nothing. The track ran parallel to the creek and a narrow blacktop road, all three of which lay in front of a row of houses. We walked past her grandparents' home, and there in the driveway was a small white car with Tennessee plates. The car that brought her here and the car that would take her away. I didn't really want to know, but I reckon I had to ask, "So, when are you going back?"

She said, "Let me see. We got here on the second, and my dad said a couple of weeks, but I heard my mom say the thirteenth or the fourteenth. They're both teachers, so they have the summer off, but they don't want to stay too long and impose."

Then I asked, "So, tell me about school, and what are your plans?"

"Oh, school is school, you know, it's high school. But I do OK, I guess. I have to work hard. My dad wants Greg and I both to go to Vanderbilt, and that's not an easy school to get in to. I'll probably end up going to a community college, like most Tennessee kids."

By this time, we had walked a quarter of a mile down the railroad track. Her brother Greg came running up behind us, and said, "Sis, I've been looking all over for you."

We both turned, and she said, "Greg, you remember Wynn."

A puzzled smile began to show on his face. "Oh yeah, I remember Wynn." As we started walking back toward the park, Greg snapped his finger and said, "I'll catch up with you two lovebirds later. I've got to grab something from the car." We walked back to the park to a swing set and each took a seat in a swing. I'm not sure where the time went, but in the snap of a finger, the sun was gone.

There was a quarter moon just above the mountain top. She said she had better be getting back to her grandparents' house, and asked if I would walk with her. We walked slowly down the track until we were directly in front of her grandparents. The moon was gone, and the only light was from the front porch light, but we continued to talk. Soon the front door opened, and a voice called out, "Denice."

She said, "I'm here, Mom, I'm just talking to my friend Wynn."

"Your friend who?"

"Wynn, Mom, I'll tell you later."

She said, "OK, but you'll have to come in soon."

I didn't sleep much that night. The next day was Sunday, and Denice and I had agreed to meet. As a family, we were as poor as a church mouse, and everyone in the area knew it. For that reason, none of the girls at school would have anything to do with me. So, I spent the night wondering how I would tell Denice. But one way or another she deserved to know, and if I put it off, it would only make things worse. I learned at an early age that I was, to say the least, short on patience. I was already sitting in the swing when I saw her walking up the tracks. As she approached me she said in her soft, Tennessee accent. "Good morning, Wynn. How was your night?"

I said, "Well, restless, to be honest with you."

She said, "Yeah, I know what you mean. I didn't sleep much either. I guess I was a little excited about today. I thought this vacation was going to be boring, and now I don't want it to end. So, what kept you awake?"

I said, "Well, I was excited about the day too, but that's not what kept me awake."

She said, "Oh? What was the problem?"

I said, "Denice, I told you I didn't have a girlfriend, and there's a reason for that. We're a large family, and neither of my parents work. We're extremely poor."

She said, "My parents are teachers. I guess we do OK, but we're certainly not rich." After that, she started talking about something else as if the subject had never been mentioned.

We must have walked ten miles that day, up and down the railroad tracks. Evening rolled around again, and it was time to say goodnight. My insecurities kicked in again and I said, Denice, "Are you sure that other thing doesn't bother you?"

She said, "What other thing? The fact that you're from a poor family? Wynn, my parents moved away from here remember? I know how things are here. I didn't come here to find a rich boyfriend, or even a boyfriend for that matter. It just happened, and neither of us know how it's going to turn out. Let's just enjoy the time we have, and not ruin it talking about things we can't change. Look, Wynn, let me see your hands." I held out my hands palms up. She took them in her own, and said, "Look at your hands, Wynn. They're callused. You're sixteen and you already have the hands of a working man. Don't you know, ambition is everything? You were born to succeed. If I didn't know that you're doing the best you can, then that would be a turnoff. Now I don't want to waste what time we have left talking about this."

My summers were spent mowing weeds with a scythe, mending fences, and helping my uncle Taube with his horses. I worked each day until about three p.m. I had problems concentrating on my work, but I didn't think it was apparent. I think it was on Thursday, when Uncle Taube and I were in a stall, working with a spirited mare. The horse suddenly jumped to the side, pinning me to the wall, knocking the breath out of me. I don't think anything was ever new under the sun, to that old man. He simply said, "Son, I think you're lovesick. Now watch what you're doing before you get trampled."

I couldn't wait to get home, bathe, dress my best and race to the community center. Those afternoons passed quickly, as we only had a few short hours each day. I was off work early on Saturday, and we had a little more time together. I remember asking if she had found out when they would be leaving. She just said, Monday or Tuesday, she wasn't sure. For a full week we had watched the waxing of the moon, and it was now at three quarters, bright and beautiful. We talked in the moonlight each night until she was called in. She would then give me a quick kiss on the cheek and the evening would end. But we were both looking forward to a full day on Sunday.

I got up early, got ready, and rushed to the community center. However, when I walked past her grandparents' house the white car was not in the driveway. I didn't think much of it, I just went to the park and took a seat in the swing. The hours dragged on and there was no sign of her. At sunset I picked up the nerve to knock at the door and ask about her. Her grandmother answered the door, and when I asked for Denice she told me the Whites were gone. She said they had not planned to leave until Tuesday, but the weatherman is predicting severe weather, so they thought they had better get back.

We didn't have a phone at home, so Denice had no way of letting me know they were leaving. The only thing I could do was go home and wait for a letter. I turned and walked back to the railroad track, and took a long look around. Funny how the world can take on a new look in an instant. Once again, I felt I had been left behind. I remembered when trainloads of coal rolled down those tracks. Now, the tracks were rusted, and weeds grew between the cross-ties. It had only been three weeks since the summer solstice, and the days were growing shorter each day. A subtle reminder that another year would soon end in Weeksbury.

Looking back, I realize how selfish I had been, to feel somehow cheated. I had just enjoyed a week of happy, blissful summer with a friend like no other. I knew Denice when we were little kids playing together on the school playground, and I thought she was the nicest kid in all the world. And for a full week she reinforced that notion. She was even more sweet and kind than I had remembered. We talked for hours during that week, in the summer of 1970. During all that time, I never heard her say a negative word about anyone or anything. She was polite and respectful regarding her family, and to me. She was a friend and a companion. I had never felt that way about anyone before, and you know... I don't believe I've felt that way about anyone since. It's dangerous for one to feel that way about someone. Dangerous because it can affect you for a lifetime.

But there were greater problems to consider. Weeksbury was dying and there was little to be done about it, and people were still dying in Vietnam. Mine was just a little adolescent sorrow that would pass unnoticed by those around me.

I got a letter from Denice about a week later, and she seemed to be as distraught as I was. Our greatest hope was in next summer, and another visit to Weeksbury. We both wrote regularly and waited patiently for the summer of 1971, and it finally came with crashing bad news. You see, her grandparents had never been to the Great Smokey Mountains near Knoxville, so this year they would visit the Whites in

Tennessee. Therefore, the Whites would not be visiting Weeksbury. The letters became less frequent after that and soon stopped completely.

There were plenty of things in the news back then. Most of it was bad news. But they say it's bad news that sells newspapers. Here are a few things that were in the news in 1970. The Beatles split up in May of that year. The crew of Apollo 13 aborted their mission and returned to Earth after a near miss with disaster. The US invaded Cambodia, sparking protests and resulting in the shooting of students at Kent State University in Ohio. Daniel Ellsberg was indicted in 1971 and sentenced to 115 years in prison for espionage when he released what was being called The Pentagon Papers. Ellsberg who was a military analyst was approached in 1968 by Secretary of Defense Robert McNamara. McNamara asked Ellsberg to give an assessment on the War in Vietnam. But the US government did not like what Ellsberg had to say and he was indicted. Ellsberg was acquitted on all charges in 1973.

Charles Manson and three of his followers were sentenced to death in 1971. However, the sentence was commuted to life in prison without parole when the state of California abolished the death penalty.

The Pittsburg Pirates won the World Series in 1971, and the Baltimore Colts won the Super Bowl.

Chapter Seventeen

I found myself sitting on a guardrail on US Route 23, about halfway between Prestonsburg and Paintsville Kentucky. I was about fifty miles from home. My uncle and aunt (Franklyn and Geneva Hall), had business in Prestonsburg and were kind enough to give me a lift to that point. Franklyn and Geneva lived about a mile from us, and I was around them a lot. They dropped me off, and Franklyn pulled into a driveway to turn around. The two of them smiled and waved as they drove away. Like so many people I've known in life, I didn't know it then, but I would never see them again.

I was hitch-hiking my way to a job in Springfield, Ohio. My brother had called earlier in the week and said he had a job for me if I could make my way to Springfield. It was a small factory, but they boasted of being the world's oldest and largest manufacturer of brooms, brushes, and mops. It was called Vining Broom. The business had been established in 1860, by

Pete and Rosie Vining. The Leventhal family had purchased the business during The Great Depression and made it into a thriving business. My brother had worked there for just over a year, and he seemed to like it.

Another car passed without stopping, but it didn't look as if they had room for another passenger anyway. I watched as a drop of sweat dropped from my nose and began to dry on the hot pavement. It sure was hot for this time of the year. It was September 1971. I probably should have been on the other side of the road, but there was no shade on that side. Behind me, the Big Sandy River had slowed to a trickle in the summer drought. Two large coal trucks flew past, and I knew they were traveling well beyond the 60 miles per hour speed limit. But at least they stirred up a breeze. It was the time of year when nature seems to take a nap. There were no birds singing, and there were times of lazy silence until another passing car. As each car passed, I listened as the sound faded and wondered where they were bound. I had way too much time to think, sitting there waiting for someone to stop.

Emil Collins had returned from Vietnam a couple of years before. He gave me his jungle boots and duffle bag. I had all my earthly possessions in that duffle bag. Another car passed, and boy was it sharp. The brake lights went all the way across the back, I thought it must have been a Thunderbird. Then a new two-tone green and white Oldsmobile Cutlass convertible passed. I turn around to look out over the river. I noticed the leaves of the sycamore trees beginning to fade in the summer heat. I was thinking that soon there would be no leaves on the trees at all. There were only a few days of summer remaining.

Just then a car horn sounded behind me. The guy in the Cutlass had backed up. "Hey," he yelled. "Are you going north?"

"Yes, I am," I replied.

"Hop in. I'm not going too far, but it might help you a little. Just throw your bag in the back seat."

I got in and said, "My name is Wynn Johnson."

He held out his hand and said, "What did you say your name was?"

I said, "It's Wynn, W Y N N."

He said, "Oh, like the baseball player, Jimmy Wynn, except that's his last name. Well, my name is Henry Ford Cantrell. Just call me Ford."

I said, "It's nice to meet you, Ford. This is a very nice car."

"Thanks, thirteen months in Vietnam paid for it. Say you look a little young to be carrying an army issue duffle bag."

"You're right, I am too young. This and the jungle boots were given to me by a friend who got out a couple of years ago."

"Was he in Nam?"

"Yes, he was, Ford. He had a tough time over there."

Ford pulled the cigarette lighter from the socket, lit a cigarette, put the lighter back into place and asked, "You smoke?"

"No, sir," I replied.

He then said, "Well it wasn't that bad for me over there. I was in a supply unit. The grunts used to call me the queer, in the rear, with the gear. But I was glad to get out of that place. Hell, on earth, in my opinion."

We had only gone a few miles when he saw something that caught his attention. He was looking to the right with a look of surprise on his face. He hit the brakes and turned onto a road where a sign read Van Leer 4 miles. He left the road and drove across a grassy field toward Van Leer Creek. There, upside down in the edge of the water was a red 1968 Ford Mustang. The car must have been there for some time. The water inside the car was about a foot deep and had already cleared, with minnows swimming in it. There were lots of footprints in the mud surrounding the car. It looked as if the people in the car had tried and failed to set it upright.

I asked, "Do you know who owns this car?"

He said, "Yeah, I think I do. A fellow by the name Trudy Tremble. He must have had his friends with him. They're a rowdy bunch of fools." He then said, "Well, let's go. Nothing we can do here. So where are you off to? And I'm sorry I forgot your name."

I said, "No problem, it happens all the time. It's Wynn, and I'm on my way to Springfield, Ohio. I've got a job waiting for me there, in a factory."

"You've got a long way to go. I've got a job with Kentucky Power and Light, starting on Monday. So, I will take you as far as Louisa, but I need to make a quick stop in Paintsville. Is that OK?"

I said, "Sure, Louisa is forty miles. That would help a lot."

In Paintsville, Ford pointed to a small drive-in restaurant on the right, called the Polar Bar. He said, "My girlfriend works there. We're getting married next summer."

He turned left onto a narrow gravel lane, crossed a wooden bridge and up a steep hill to the last house in a row of four. All four houses were post World War Two and were exactly alike. They were white, one story, with full-length porches across the front overlooking the town. The lane passed in front of the houses, and a row of hedge bushes separated the lane from the yards.

Ford got out and began to part through the branches of the hedge bushes as if he were looking for something. I hadn't noticed the dark cloud that had appeared above the mountain to the rear of the houses. Suddenly, large raindrops began to fall. Ford scrambled to close the convertible's top. He then continued his search. Just then the screen door slammed and there was a loud belch. An older gentleman, with white disheveled hair and a rather thick waist, stepped onto the porch. He set a wine bottle on the railing, and asked, "This what you're looking for?"

Ford said, "Yeah, Grandpa, that's it."

The old man said, "Well you're too late. The content of this bottle is already in my gut."

Ford said, "Grandpa! You said you quit drinking alcohol."

The old man said, "I did not say I quit drinking alcohol, I said I quit buying it."

These houses stood on a hill to the west, and above the town of Paintsville. Looking across the valley to the east and north, I could see waves of rain and bright sunshine at the same time. There was a low rumble of thunder, but it was nothing more than a fast-moving shower.

Ford hurried toward the steps leading to the front porch. As he did he yelled over his left shoulder, "Roll your window up and come on up here. I want you to meet this guy."

I got out and rushed up the steps to the porch. The old man didn't stand but he put out his hand and asked, "Now, what's your name?"

I said, "Wynn Johnson."

He said, "Win? What the hell kind of name is that?"

I said, "I don't know. I'm not sure I know how to answer that."

Ford said, "Now tell him your own name, Grandpa, and don't give him a hard time."

The old man said, "My name is Sam Houston Cantrell."

He invited me to sit, but just then there was a racket down below as a car slid to a halt in the gravel parking lot of the Polar Bar. A man jumped out of the car and started running for his life. He didn't even look for traffic as he bolted across Highway 23. He was a tall lanky fellow with a scraggly looking beard. And even though it was a sweltering day, he was wearing a long sleeve flannel shirt and tan colored trousers that were about a foot too short. The man looked for all the world like Shaggy from the *Scooby-Doo* cartoon Show on TV. It would have been a little out of his way to have gone to the bridge, so he headed straight for the creek. I'm sure the poor fool would have been better off barefooted. I swear to you he was trying to run an all-out foot-race in flip-flops.

Suddenly another car slid to a halt. This one was a Johnson County Sheriff's Deputy who jumped out of his car and started after the first man. Until now I thought old Sam Houston was too drunk to stand, but he jumped to his feet with excitement and said. "What's this? The law's after Trudy. Ruuun, Trudy Tremble. You're goanna get cetched." The old man watched with great interest, then called out again. "The law's after you, Trudy, you're goanna get cetched."

149

Trudy made it to the creek and splashed on through, but it slowed him down considerably and the officer was gaining on him. By then, I realized Trudy was headed for the house next door. We could hear their heavy breathing as the chase started up the hill. The old man continued to encourage the runner. "He's gaining on you, Trudy. You're goanna get cetched. Try to make it to the house, Trudy, before you get cetched."

The steep hill was becoming a struggle for both men now, but the one being chased was having the most difficulty. My guess is that he might have been a little tipsy, which is probably why the sheriff was after him. It might also have been because Trudy's car was upside down in the creek or both. The deputy was within ten feet of Trudy now and just when I thought the race was over, Trudy had one last burst of speed. I guess he thought he would be safe from the law if he made it into the house. The sheriff was only about ten feet behind Trudy as old Sam Houston continued to cheer. "Hurry, Trudy, he's a gaining on you." Trudy made it to the steps and bounded them two at a time. The painted wood floor of the porch was wet from the rain and when Trudy's feet hit that floor, he lost control. His feet spread apart, and he did a cheer-leader's split as he crumpled into the screen door.

The old sheriff was on him immediately. He picked Trudy up from the floor, handcuffed him, turned him around facing the way they had come. The deputy then gave Trudy a swift kick in the backside, looked over at us and said, "Boys, it sure is hot today." With that, he led Trudy back down the hill.

Old Sam wouldn't let it go. He was laughing loudly as he yelled, "I told you, Trudy, you was a goanna get cetched."

As we left the old man on the porch and drove away, he snapped to attention and saluted. He held that salute until we were out of sight. I said to Ford, "You know, your grandfather's quite a character."

Ford said, "Yeah, I know. The old son of a bitch is an atheist too. He fought in the thickest of battles in the First World War. He'll be quick to tell you that virgin birth is impossible."

I said, "Well, that would be an empty way to live your life."

Ford said, "I know, but there's no changing him."

Driving north on 23, Ford said, "It's going to be tough getting a ride through Ashland during rush hour. From about three to six. Ashland Oil, Armco Steel, C&O Railroad, they're all getting off work. They're all in a hurry to get home and they're not going to stop for you. Take my advice and hop a train, ride it to West Portsmouth and go north on 104."

I said, "Well, it sounds easy enough, but how do I do that?"

He said, "I'll show you. I told you I'm going to be working for Kentucky Power and Light at the Louisa power plant. Well, I've gotten to know some of those guys. They told me things like how much power is generated there, how much coal they use and so forth. A train drops a couple of coal cars there about three times a week and then they go on to a plant near Cincinnati. These old coal trains don't move very fast anyway. You can get on a northbound at the Louisa plant and ride it through Ashland, Greenup, and Portsmouth. They'll slow down to a crawl through Portsmouth. They'll start picking up speed when they get to West Portsmouth. You'd better jump off along 104 or you'll end up in Cincinnati. From there you'll want to go north on 104."

Ford slowed down as we drove past the power plant. He pointed and said, "See the train with the two Diesels pointed north? That's the one you're going to want to be on. And you're in luck, they're pulling some flat-cars. I'll turn around and take you back and drop you off at the end of the train. You can sneak through the weeds and get on the last car. There shouldn't be too much dust flying around on the last car when the train starts rolling."

The train was about a quarter of a mile long. Ford drove me back to the south where we could see the end. I thanked him for the ride and the experience. I walked down an embankment, through some tall weeds, crossed four sets of tracks to the last car on the train. I was scared stiff. I was sure that some big, burly brakeman would see me and know what I was up to. But I climbed onto the flat-car and made myself comfortable. That's when I realized that everything I touched was coated with coal dust. The cream-colored corduroy pants I had on would soon be black.

Once again, I had time to think. The Big Sandy River flows north out of the mountains, picking up tributaries along the way, and empties into the Ohio River near Ashland. I was forty miles north of where I was when Ford picked me up and almost a hundred miles from home. The river ran just on the other side of the tracks and behind the power plant. It was still a lazy river, but much wider and much deeper. I felt naked sitting there on that train car. The tracks were parallel and about a hundred yards from US 23. Passersby on that highway could have seen me and probably did.

I had been sitting there for over an hour in the hot sun and, just when I was about to give up, there was a violent bump and the train began to move slowly. The movement created a gentle breeze that felt good on my face and arms. My greatest fear was being seen when the car I was on passed in front of the power plant. What I didn't know then was that the workers at the plant worked inside the building. There would be no one outside to see me. But I breathed a little easier when the plant was behind me and the train picked up speed.

There was absolutely nothing to hide me from the world as I sat there on that flat-car. At crossings, impatient drivers hurried across the tracks without noticing me as the last car cleared the crossings. In about half an hour we entered the city of Catlettsburg and I could smell the Ashland Oil refinery. It was not an unpleasant smell, but one that filled the air for miles around. It was much like the smell of hot asphalt. I could see the confluent where the Big Sandy River flowed into the Ohio River.

Beginning with Catlettsburg, then Ashland, Russell, Worthington, then Greenup, those towns were linked together along the south bank of the Ohio River. This was a stretch of about forty miles where the train moved at a snail's pace. US 23 was the main drag through Ashland, running parallel to the railroad track and the river. As the train rolled through the business district, people in business clothes hurried across the tracks when the train passed. Some pointed and yelled when they saw me, others smiled and waved, while some paid no attention at all.

The train was still creeping along when it cleared Greenup. A man raking grass clippings in a yard that obviously had not been mowed in a long time yelled, "I see you on that there train, boy. And you're goanna get kicked off, iffan you get cetched."

I waved to the man and told him I worked for the railroad. He yelled something else which I couldn't make out. I yelled back, "Shut up and take care of your yard." But I'm sure he didn't hear me either.

The mountains had become hills now, and there was a lot more distance between them. It must have been at least five miles from the hills of northern Kentucky, to the hills of southern Ohio. The Ohio River stretched seemingly endless to the east and to the west dividing Kentucky and Ohio. Another half an hour or so and the train crossed a long bridge into the city of Portsmouth Ohio. I began to see things that I had only seen on TV. There was a McDonald's restaurant, and a BBF with their signature sign of the twirling satellite. The BBF restaurant chain boasted the best burger in America, soon to become Burger Sheff, soon to become Hardees.

The train was moving in a northwest direction now, and I could tell the day was coming to an end. Just a few more miles and I would have to get off that train. Once again, the train entered open country, and there was a two-lane highway running parallel to the tracks. I was certain that was Route 104, and when the train began to pick up speed, I jumped. I landed well clear of the tracks in the weeds and gravel. I felt a profound sense of accomplishment as I picked up my duffle bag and walked toward the road.

I looked to the west and realized why the day had become dark. The sun had not gone down but was hidden by a dark gray storm cloud. It had been a hot, dry summer, and under other circumstances a cooling thunderstorm would have been welcome. The rolling hills of the Scioto River Valley were now miles apart. Ripening grain was turning yellow and almost ready for harvesting in the fields along the road.

As I walked along that road I began to daydream. This was a land rich in history. A place of tribal wars and competition between a stone-aged people who lived and farmed this rich valley for thousands of years. It is a place where George Rogers Clark and his Long Knives drove the tribes of the Shawnee, Mingo, and the Piqua north and west into Canada. A place where the mighty Tecumseh dove to the bottom of the Scioto River in mid-winter to prove his worthiness to be chief and statesman of the Shawnee.

The dark clouds were moving closer and I thought I saw a faint flicker of lightning. My guess would be that the storm would be here in less than an hour. My hope was to find a bridge or an overpass for shelter till the storm passed. I don't think I could have walked any faster, yet I seemed to be getting nowhere. *My God, the world is big,* I thought to myself. If I had an hour before the storm, I could probably walk another four to six miles. Surely, I could find a place to shelter by then.

It had been an incredibly lazy summer day walking past those houses and farms of southern Ohio. There were some freshly fallen poplar leaves scattered along the roadside. Probably not the result of autumn but the effects of the summer heat. However, the corn was turning brown, especially the leaves closest to the ground, and that was definitely a promise of autumn. A cool breeze swept in from the west, preceding the storm. The corn squeaked and rattled in the breeze. A couple of crows cawed and took off for wherever they go to shelter during a storm. Lightning flashed again, and this time it was brighter and closer. It was obvious to me that this lazy summer day was about to take on a different look. Then I heard a low rumble of thunder and I knew the time was short before the storm.

About twenty minutes later the first raindrops began to fall. I was bracing for the worst when a car passed me, then pulled to the side of the road. The car was a white Ford Galaxy, probably a 1966 or 67 model. I rushed to the car and a man's voice said, "Need a ride?"

I crawled into the back seat and apologized for my clothes being so dirty. I told them I had fallen down an embankment, which was half true. They were a middle-aged couple, perhaps a little on the heavy side. They introduced themselves as George and Carol Wilson. They said they were on their way to Jamestown, and asked where I was heading. I told them Springfield and the man said, "Well, that's only another twenty miles or so north of Jamestown."

I thanked them for the ride and told them a short version of my story. They invited me to put my window down as the air conditioning didn't work. There was something pleasant in those days when people didn't travel with windows closed tightly in air-conditioned comfort. In those days when you passed a hog farm, you smelled a hog farm. You smelled the exhausts of other vehicles, the dead animals, and anything else that produced a smell. But there were pleasant smells and fresh air as well.

Shortly after they picked me up, we approached the town of Chillicothe and its paper mill. Mead Paper Company had made their home in Chillicothe for many years. They employed a lot of people and produced a lot of paper. But the smokestack of that plant produced a totally unpleasant smell that drifted for miles in every direction. It was a smell much like burned sauerkraut. I said I wondered if the folks nearby ever got used to the smell. George said, "I doubt it. Sometimes, we can smell it in Jamestown, and that's forty or fifty miles away."

We reached a major intersection where a sign read, US 23 North to Columbus, and another sign read, Dayton Next Left. George turned the car left onto Highway 35 west. Soon we were passing through Washington Court House. The wind had shifted, giving way to some pleasant smells through that small town. There was the smell of food from local restaurants, the smell of fresh mowed grass, and burning charcoal. Carol said to George, "Whoever is cooking on the grill better move it into the garage or something. This rain's getting harder."

George said, "Yeah, we'd better roll up the windows." It was well after dark when we got to Jamestown. The storm turned out to be nothing more than a summer thunderstorm, with about fifteen minutes of downpour. However, the rain was still falling at a steady pace.

George stopped at the center of Jamestown, at the intersection of Highway 35 and Highway 72. He looked over his right shoulder and said, "Well, partner, we're turning left here, and you need to go right."

His wife said, "Wait a minute, honey. Let's not put him out in the rain. It's only twenty miles or so, let's run him up there."

I said, "Listen, folks, you've done enough already. I'm sure I can make it from here."

George looked at his wife as if he hadn't heard a word I said. He said to her, "I guess that'd be all right."

With that he turned the car to the right and headed north on Highway 72, where a sign read Springfield 21 Miles. He looked at me in the rearview mirror and said, "Son, you'd never be able to get a ride on this road at night. Where exactly are you going?"

I said, "I'm going to 425 North Burnett Road."

He said, "Yeah, I know where Burnett Road is. It runs in front of Community Hospital." The rain had almost stopped when George and Carol dropped me off at the address. I expressed my gratitude and waved as they drove away.

The house was a Victorian style two-story house which had been divided into three efficiency apartments. My sister Lily and her husband Bill lived upstairs, my brother Ernie and his wife Judy lived downstairs. There was an even smaller apartment on the first floor where a single hippie lived. I say hippie because he had enough hair and beard on him to stuff a pillow. He drove a Volkswagen van covered in peace signs, and there was the occasional smell of pot coming through the walls.

There was a wooden screen door and it was slightly ajar, and when I knocked it made a much louder sound than I expected. Ernie opened the door in his pajamas, and he looked very tired. I apologized for the loud knock and for waking him. He said, "It's no problem. You'll soon learn, it's early to bed, early to rise in the blue-collar world. Come on, I'll show you where everything is."

My room was on the north side of the house next to the alley. The room had been an open porch, but enclosed for living space when the house was divided into apartments. Ernie said, "The plant is about three-quarters of a mile straight down that road. The man you need to talk to won't be in until after nine. When you're ready just come on down."

I went to bed, but I was too wound up to sleep. I was two hundred and fifty miles from where I had slept last night, and it seemed like a whole new world. I was a little nervous about the day ahead. Then I started thinking about everything that had taken place on the way here. I thought about Trudy Tremble, and I began to chuckle. The next thing I heard sounded like the whistle of an ocean liner.

Chapter Eighteen

I knew it was early, and I wanted to sleep just a little while longer, but the steamship whistle sounded again about fifteen minutes later, so I got up. I showered, got dressed, and walked out to the street. It was a pretty place. The street and alley were lined with large maple trees. There were large two-story houses and one-story cottages, all of them white. Most of them had fenced yards. Looking down the alley to the west I could see the golden arches of a McDonald's restaurant. Beyond that was a convenience store called Lawsons. I could see this new life had its conveniences.

It was almost eight, so I thought I'd better walk on down to the plant. There had been a lot of traffic earlier, but now the streets were quiet. I didn't see anyone in the yards either. It was a time when children went to school, dad went to work, and mom took care of the home.

It was downhill all the way to Vining's plant. The air that morning was smoky, and there was a familiar smell. I remembered that smell from spring days when we raked last year's cornstalks into a pile and burned them. No question about it, there could be no other smell. I got within sight of the factory and saw a smokestack on the back of the building with blue smoke rising from it. I realized that's where the smell was coming from.

I walked into the building, where Ernie met me and led me to a small office. He introduced me to a gentleman by the name of John Payton. I don't remember filling out an application or signing any papers. After a short interview, he said to my brother, "Take him to Bob Chambliss and he'll show him what to do." I followed Ernie into the production area, where the noise was incredible. There was no air conditioning, but there was a large ventilation system which kept the air moving throughout the building. The smell was like that of cornstalks drying in the sun, and there was a pale green dust that coated the place.

Ernie leaned in close to me and said, "Careful of this Bob Chambliss. He's a mean old SOB. I think if he smiled his face would break."

Bob Chambliss was an older fellow, who looked slightly beyond retirement age. He wasn't very tall, but carried himself like the meanest high school coach you ever met. He didn't look up or offer a handshake, he only pointed, and with a dry, gruff voice he said, "That fellow over there's name is Walter Wells. He'll show you how to run that scraper."

When we approached, Walter stepped back away from the machine in order to hear what we were saying. Ernie said, "Walt, this is my brother. Will you show him the ropes?"

Walter said, "Sure, I can use the help."

Walter pushed a rack which held ten dozen brooms to the right of the scraper. He said, "The first thing you're going to learn is the basic material in these brooms. These brooms are made of broom corn. The broom corn plant looks and smells just like the corn plant you're familiar with. The difference with this kind of corn is that instead of an ear of corn, there's a wisp of straw. At breaktime, walk out to the back dock, there's some growing from seeds that have been spilled. Now, look at the brooms I'm working on. These are made of a kind of shredded cacti called sotol, we call it grass. Now be careful with this stuff. It'll cut you like a knife."

Just then Bob Chambliss walked over and said, "Well, are you going to talk all day or scrape some brooms?"

There were two scrapers, and they were designed to remove seeds and tangles from the brooms before they were flattened and sewn in a machine called a stitcher. Scrapers were belt-driven wooden drums which resembled whiskey barrels with rows of butter knives protruding from them. My job was to take the brooms one at a time from the rack and hold on the spinning drum until the seeds and tangles were gone. When the brooms first touched the drum, there was a quick pull. One had to be careful not to be caught off balance and pulled onto the drum. No one asked, and I didn't tell anyone I was only seventeen.

The first thing I noticed about that way of life was that time passed quickly. It was a beautiful autumn, but with the old plant's frosted glass windows it was never brighter inside than a foggy day. Ernie and I worked until noon on Saturdays, and it was such a joy to stroll home in the early afternoon sun.

General George Rogers Clark had built his mansion on a hill just a few miles west of town early in the nineteenth century. The house and grounds had been purchased by Springfield and made into a city park. There was a lake with walking trails and a waterfall that was hidden from most of the world. Bill would take us there for picnics on Sundays. We strolled along the trails, each one of us secretly hoping that the day would never end. But alas, one Sunday the leaves on the trees were beautiful, the next Sunday the leaves were beautiful but on the ground.

It was hard work, but I would, as they say, "get into it" and daydream the time away. It was mid-October on a Thursday just before lunch break, I had become complacent. I wasn't holding the broom handle tightly enough when it hit the drum. The handle slipped through my hands sending a splinter through the web of my left hand. On the top of my hand, the point of the splinter was sharp and about the size of a small knife blade. On the inside of my hand, it was the size of a carpenter's pencil.

I was in agonizing pain, but I didn't know what to do. I was afraid if anyone found out, I would be fired for operating the machine at seventeen years old. I asked Walter if he had a pair of plyers. He went to the maintenance man and came back with a pair. I tried to pull the slab from my hand, but it broke off at the surface, and the pain increased.

In addition to the physical pain, I felt stupid. Ernie kept telling me it was just an accident, but I was so afraid of losing my job for being too young to operate the machine. Minimum wage in 1971 was $1.25 per hour. I was making $1.70 per hour and with my age, and lack of experience, I knew I couldn't replace that job. It was a time when a lot of men were still in Vietnam and a lot of factories in town needed help. I was sure if I tried to get another job, they would ask for more than I had to offer in age, education, and experience.

It was a long and sleepless night. All I could think about was my hand and my job. If I had thought crying would've helped, I would have wept. I liked the job, and if not for President Nixon's price and wage freeze, I would be getting another ten cents on the hour. I tried to keep my mind off the pain, but it was impossible. I thought about the pain Christ must have felt, nailed to a cross and left hanging from those nails. How on earth was I going to be able to work and yet keep my secret? The only plan I could come up with was to bandage the wound and do the best I could. After what seemed to be an endless night, I heard Ernie's knock at the door letting me know that it was time to go to work.

I could hardly bend my hand that morning. Ernie was seven years older and several years wiser. He said to me, "You've got to get that slab out of your hand."

I said, "I know. I hope that when the infection forms around it I'll be able to pull it out."

He said, "That's not the way it works. The swelling will tighten around it and make it worse."

The steamship whistle sounded as we walked into the plant, which was sounding from the International Harvester plant next door. Vining had its own loud buzzer to begin and end work shifts. It was 07:00. I stuck my time card into the clock and punched in, took a deep breath and said to myself, "*I can do this.*"

I made it until just before lunch and the pain was becoming unbearable. I saw Bob Chambliss walking toward me and I thought, *Well, this is it.* The old man said to me, "Wynn, you see that black guy up there on the dock? He's going to take you up to Community Hospital. You tell them to take that slab out of your hand

and send the bill to Vining Broom." With that, he just turned and walked away.

I walked up to the guy on the dock and he said to me, "Come on, man, I'm your ambulance driver. My name's Robert Clark. Just call me Clarkie." I told him my name, and he said, "So how do you spell that, W I N?"

I said, "No, it's W Y N N."

Clarkie drove a large Oldsmobile, with some kind of fuzzy covering on the dash, front, back and on the steering wheel. He was listening to a soul music station out of Dayton. Robert Clark was a handsome fellow. He had nice skin tone and a perfect smile. The man could have passed for Marvin Gaye's twin, complete with a soft smooth voice, as he sang along with the radio.

He pulled into the emergency room entrance and said, "All right, man, I'll be in the parking lot just around the corner of the building."

I checked in at the nurse's station and took a seat. It was only about ten minutes later when my name was called. The doctor looked at my hand and shook his head. "When did this happen?" he asked.

I said, "Yesterday morning."

He said, "Then why didn't you come in yesterday?" Then he said, "Let's get you numbed up." The pain was gone almost immediately. They had my arm through a curtain and I was unable to see what they were doing. It didn't take more than fifteen minutes or so, and I was being taken to the front entrance in a wheelchair. Hospital policy, I guess.

I found Robert with the seat back as far as it would go, and he looked to be snoozing. When I opened the car door he stretched, yawned and said, "Dang, I thought it would take longer." It was a beautiful day just after noon when we drove north on Burnett Road. We stopped for the red light at Columbus Road but instead of driving straight through the light and into Vining's parking lot, Clarkie made a right turn and headed east.

I said to him, "You're confusing me, sir."

He said, "What do you mean? Don't tell me you're in a hurry to go back in that place?"

I said, "No, but I don't want to lose my job."

He said, "Relax. They have no way of knowing how long this would take."

He drove east on Columbus Road for a mile or so then turned left. There was a brown sign on the right which read, City of Springfield, Reed Park. It was obvious the narrow lane had once been a railroad. Both sides were lined with large sycamore trees, and straight ahead was a steel bridge where many trains had once crossed. To the right was a pasture with a few cows. I hadn't realized how close I was to the edge of town.

On the other side of the bridge, the lane took a sharp right. Shortly after that, he took another sharp right turning into a gravel parking area. There was a river flowing directly in front of us. The water flowed over a small dam just before it passed under the steel bridge.

On the other side of the river, a young mother splashed in the water with her children. I asked Clarkie what river it was, and he said, "That's Buck Creek. It looks peaceful now, but when that thing floods, wow, look out. They're building a big reservoir about a mile upstream. They say they'll be able to control flooding as far away as Dayton. That's thirty miles from here."

It was one thirty in the afternoon and I kept thinking I should be back at work. Clarkie reached under the seat and pulled out a small, black bag. I was oblivious to drugs, but I knew exactly what he was going to do. I got out of the car and walked over to sit on a picnic table. Clarkie said, "What's the matter with you? Get back in the car and relax, there's no cops around here." I stayed where I was, and he turned on the radio, then joined me at the picnic table. He said, "Man you got to loosen up, everybody smokes pot."

I said, "Well, I don't, I don't even smoke cigarettes."

He said, "I don't smoke cigarettes either. Cigarettes will kill you."

I asked, "How long have you worked at Vining, Clarkie?"

He said, "Just over two years. I started just after I got back from Vietnam."

I said, "Oh, you were over there?"

He said, "Oh yeah, there's quite a few of us who came home and got a job there. Vining's good about hiring vets. Let's see, there's Bill Beufels, he's the other black guy. Charlie Mathews, Bill Donohoe, Dallas Fairchild, and John Parkston; that I know of. Those last two are messed up."

I asked, "What do you mean, messed up?"

He said, "Well, you notice they don't talk much. John Parkston, he's from somewhere up on the U-P of Michigan. He and Ed Leventhal, you know, the nephew of the owners. They met in college, somewhere up around Cleveland. Ed, he taught school for a while before he started working here, and Parkston, he wanted to be a pilot. He was flying an F-4 Phantom Jet. He was in Vietnam when he got blasted with a SAM. You know, a surface to air missile. He ejected, but it messed him up, you know? Emotionally. Ed got a letter from his folks, asking if John could work at Vining till he got his act straight.

"Dallas, he's a good guy. He'll talk to you one on one, but he gets nervous in a crowd. That's how he lost an eye, you know. He's a smart kid, but like you, like me, he doesn't have it on paper. And when you don't have an education in Vietnam, you are what they call a BBS. Basic bullet stopper. That place is incredibly dark at night. He was on patrol and he was too close to the point man. You know, the guy in the lead. That point man stepped on a bouncing betty. A piece of shrapnel passed through Dallas's temple, behind his right eye. I think what messed up Dallas the most was the point man. That point man didn't have anything left from the bellybutton down, but he lived long enough to say goodbye. He asked Dallas to say so long to his folks, and tell them not to worry, he'd be OK.

"Ever notice all those bloody paper towels in the men's room at work? Well, anyway, they're from Dallas. He bleeds about a pint from his nose every morning. I'll bet it's from that weed killer, agent orange." I just sat there listening as Clarkie continued to tell me about our co-workers.

"You know that tall, bald-headed, older fellow who works on the dock, his name is Horace Price? Well, his son-in-law worked here before he joined the service. I hear old Price's daughter was bad news. I didn't know his son-in-law personally, but at Vining everyone knows everything about everybody. I guess the two of them never got along to begin with, and probably should have never been married. One day they had a fight, and he just up and joined the army. They shipped him to Vietnam.

"Not more than six months after he went in, an artillery round hit close to him. He had severe brain damage, he probably would have been better off if he'd died there on the spot. They brought that boy home and put him in a nursing home down in Xenia. He laid there and suffered for six or seven months before he died.

According to Bob Stallings, the boy's wife was out being a whore while he was slowly dying. Sounds like the only thing she wanted was that SGLI. You know, Servicemen's Group Life Insurance. Well, they say she blew through that twenty thousand bucks in a hurry."

I said, "How about Charlie Mathews? Did he get messed up over there?"

Clarkie laughed and said, "No, he was messed up before he went there. He's an OK guy. He's just a little goofy. Almost all the men at Vining were in the service, including the owners, Fred and Harry Leventhal. They both served during the Second World War in Europe. Imagine being a Jew, and sent to fight in Europe during that war. Fred was an enlisted man, a sergeant in the army. Harry was an officer, he was a captain in the army. Bob Stallings was in the Navy. He served in the South Pacific. Thurman Fugate fought in Europe. Don Craycraft, he fought with the Marines in Korea. Roy Kelly (the assistant plant manager), he served in Korea just after the war. They're all a pretty good bunch of guys. But don't let them boss you around, that's just how those old military guys are."

There was not a cloud in the sky that entire day, just a couple of long white lines across the sky from the jets. A noisy flock of ducks quacked and played in the water, and for a moment I forgot all about Vining. Springfield was an industrial town, with forty-thousand men and women toiling in the factories as Clarkie and I sat there relaxing on a picnic table.

I said, "Clarkie, we'd better get on back; it's almost three."

He lit what was left of the joint and sucked the smoke between his fingers. I'm not sure how he did it without burning himself. He held the joint until he knew it was out, then dropped it back into the bag. He stood up and said, "OK, if we must."

Robert Clark and I had only spent a few hours together, but I could tell we were going to be friends. He accepted the fact that I didn't smoke pot and didn't intend to start. I accepted the fact that he did smoke it and didn't intend to quit. He did continue to try and convince me that pot was harmless.

I lay in bed that night thinking about everything that had happened that day and I just couldn't sleep. There were a lot of freight trains that passed through Springfield, and where we lived was right in the middle of it. Until you got used to it, those trains would wake you faster than you could fall asleep. If a train was headed east, the sound would begin with a faint whistle in the direction my head was pointing. The sound would become louder and the sound of the engines could be heard. Then the train sounded as if it were to my left at the loudest point. As the sound began to fade it seemed to be in the direction my feet were pointing, then to my right as it faded completely. It sounded as if the trains were making a complete circle. The opposite occurred when a train was headed west.

I used to lie there and wonder where those trains were going. If they were headed west, I imagined perhaps, Dayton, Cincinnati, Indianapolis or Saint Louis. If they were headed east, I thought they might be headed for Columbus, Pittsburg, or Philadelphia. Then I thought about home and wondered what the folks there were doing.

I had seen a lot of good times growing up there, but I had seen some horrible times as well. It's funny, how one horrible event can erase tons of good ones. I still think leaving was my only choice, and it allowed me to view Weeksbury from the outside. To see what, if anything, changed without me. I was sure my leaving would go unnoticed.

Vining had a small break room with tables and chairs, but not everyone used it. There were two local taverns which served home-style meals to factory workers for two dollars and fifty cents. They were the Blue Diamond Grill and the Elmar Bar, and they were both within walking distance. But my brother Ernie, Clarkie and I just hung out on the dock at lunchtime when the weather was nice.

Chapter Nineteen

Clarkie knew just about everything about everyone who worked there. He also told us he was going to marry Tracy Black, the only problem was, Tracy didn't know it. Clarkie was a handsome man, but I thought he had his sights set way too high. Tracy was a striking black lady, and as looks go she was perfect. She had a bright and bubbly personality, she loved to laugh, and she loved to smile. I didn't think he stood a chance, but he strolled right up to her in front of us all, and said, "Tracy, I want you to marry me."

Tracy just laughed and said, "Sure, but you'd better be good to me. I have nine sisters and we'll kick your butt." They didn't waste any time, they were married two weeks later. Tracy did indeed have nine sisters, and they were all pretty. I thought about what beautiful children they would have, but to my knowledge, they never had any.

Walter Wells was born and raised in Virgie Kentucky, the place where I was born. I didn't think there was anyone else in the state of Ohio who knew where Virgie Kentucky was located. He had lived and worked there as a coal miner. He even mentioned a few people who I had known. Walter never missed a day of work. He was always on time, and never gave less than one hundred percent when he was on the job.

On the twenty-fifth anniversary of his hire date, Ed Leventhal (the general manager) walked over and handed Walter a shiny new wristwatch. Walter tried to downplay his emotions, but I could tell he was proud of that watch. He admired it for a couple of minutes, then went back to work. As the days passed, I noticed Walter twisting at the stem, shaking the watch, then holding it to his ear. I asked him if he was having trouble with the watch, and he said, "It's not worth a damn. Every time I try to wind it, I get the time all messed up."

I took the watch and stepped to where I could see the clock on the other side of the plant. I set the time, pushed the stem back in and said to him, "Don't try to wind it, Walt, it's quartz, you don't have to wind it."

He said he had never heard of a watch that didn't have to be wound, but when it worked, he was proud of it. He wore summer shirts so that when he took off his coat, he didn't have to raise his sleeve to show it to his friends.

Vining had some colorful characters working for them. One of these characters was a woman by the name Dorothy. I will not reveal her last name for fear that I might upset her relatives. She was in her late fifties then, and as that's been almost half of a century ago, I'm sure she's resting peacefully in her grave. I guess the only thing that made her interesting was the fact that she was just plain mean. And what made her even meaner was that most people called her Dot. Dorothy was another dedicated employee, but if you asked her for the time of day, she would tell you, "It's time for you to get an f—ing watch." Even the bosses avoided having a conversation with her.

Dorothy was not much more than four feet tall and almost as wide. She had short frizzy hair and wore thick glasses. The glasses gave her that Harry Truman sort of look. The glasses made her eyes look huge. At least I thought it was the glasses. My guess is that she had been mean and ugly for so long, the ugliness had become permanent.

She lived close by and walked to work each day. To keep her from standing in the cold till the place opened, Walter let her sit with him in his car. At least I thought that was the reason she was sitting in Walter's car. The fact that the car windows were always steamed up didn't stir my curiosity.

One morning as I was walking through the parking lot, a woman stepped from behind the corner of the building with a club in her hand. With the windows all steamed up, I'm sure they didn't see her coming. The woman walked straight to Walter's car and slammed that club across the top. She yelled in a strong manly voice, "You get that nasty old bitch out of my car."

Dorothy jumped out of the car, clenched her fists and asked, "What the f—'s going on." And, with that, she started toward the woman.

The woman with the club was Walter's wife who drew the club back like a golfer preparing to tee off, and said, "Come on, you ugly old bitch."

Dorothy didn't say another word. She headed for the front door of the plant, straightening her clothes and trying to make herself presentable. Walter got out as well and started toward the side door of the plant. His wife said, "You get your sorry, skinny ass back in that car."

Walter humbly replied, "OK."

It was lunchtime, and Walter still hadn't come in from the parking lot. I was sure he had gone home for the day. I walked up to the front dock to see if his car was still there. It was, there was steam coming from the tail-pipe and the car was rocking slightly. Just then, the driver's side door flew open and Walter was shoved from the car. I saw the rather large foot and leg, that had pushed Walter from the car, disappear back into the car. The car door closed, the window came down, and I could hear the woman yelling as she shook her fist and sped away.

Charlie Ballenger is our next colorful subject. To my knowledge, he never had a living soul but himself. He was said to have come from somewhere in Kentucky. He just showed up sometime in the mid-1940s and went to work. His title was Bleach Man. There was a large concrete container that was filled with water, and a green dye was added to enhance the color and soften the materials for the brooms. The dye was in the form of leaf-green crystals, and it only took a sprinkling to color the five-hundred-gallon concrete container filled with water. The bales of material were lowered into and out of the colored water with a chain hoist. If the colored water came in contact with your skin, it could take days, or even weeks, to remove it.

Charlie was careful to keep the dye from his head and neck, but his clothes, shoes and everything else about him was green. The poor guy, he didn't seem to mind. He lived clear over on the west side of town, but he rode a bicycle to work. But it was no ordinary bicycle. He had so many lights, horns, stickers, and other decorations on it that when he rode it he looked like a circus act. That bicycle was the only thing he had in the world. And if the snow was too deep, he walked to work and pushed the bicycle through the snow.

No one knew that Charlie had an eye for Dorothy, until he found out about the "parking lot love triangle."

Charlie wasn't mad at Walter, but he was furious with Dorothy. The women's restroom and the water fountain were next to the bleach room where Charlie worked. At the end of the day, Dorothy came out of the restroom and stopped at the fountain for a long drink of water. Charlie passed behind her with a small measuring cup and sprinkled green bleach onto the back of Dorothy's head and neck. Dorothy never caught on to the prank. She just stormed from the building in her usual way. She must have taken a much-needed shower that night, for when she showed up the next morning she was as green as grass over the septic system.

Folks started calling her the wicked witch of the west, and she became even meaner. In the days and weeks, it took to wear off, Dorothy didn't place anything anywhere. She pitched, threw, and slammed everything she touched. Her fresh, new look killed Charlie's affection, and he never spoke to her again. Dorothy was never sure it was Charlie who gave her that look, but she had her suspicions. Charlie couldn't prove anything either, but he must have had ten flat tires on that bicycle after the run-in with Dorothy.

Charlie lived in a boarding house, at the mercy of a nasty old land-lady. She took every dollar the old guy made, in return for a bed and two sandwiches per day. I say old guy because no one was sure just how old Charlie was, and he didn't know. It was obvious that he had lived a hard life.

He had served a short term in the army, but there was something that just wasn't right with him. He liked to talk, and when there was no one around, he had two-way conversations with himself. He was never taught to read or write, and I just don't think anyone ever took the time to teach him the simplest things in life.

When he was able to steal from gardens or apple trees, he just didn't come to work. When the fruits and vegetables were no longer in season, he was a faithful employee. No one was sure where he lived until one day, when he hadn't been seen for days, he was spotted by Eugene Fitch. According to Fitch, Charlie was standing on the porch of a burning house. He was sipping coffee from a large cup and having one of his two-way conversations with himself as if nothing was wrong. I think that was the last I heard of Charlie.

Chapter Twenty

Vining had two winos working there, they were Chester George and Bill Dunbar. No one was ever sure if or when those two would show up for work. But if they were not at work, it was a safe bet that they were together somewhere. They were as they say, "birds of a feather." Chester was in his early forties. He was not a bad looking guy, but he had turned drunk after a couple of bad marriages. He was average size, and intelligent when he was sober.

Clarkie and I walked into the Blue Diamond grill for lunch one day and saw Chester asleep at a table. The bartender called to us, "Hey, do you guys know that drunk passed out at the table?"

Clarkie said, "We know him."

The bartender said, "Could you guys get him out of here before I lose my liquor license?"

Clarkie said, "How'd he get here?"

The bartender said, "He drove that old Buick parked around the side of the building. He was here waiting when I opened this morning, and he was already drunk then."

As we were dragging Chester through the side door, Clarkie said, "What's this guy doing driving? He hasn't had a license in years. If he gets caught, he'll go to jail for a long time. It's funny how guys like him let petty things like this grow into monsters." We didn't want him to wake up behind the wheel, so we placed him in the back seat of the old Buick. We took the car keys from his pocket and asked the bartender to hold them until Chester woke up, sobered up, or both.

Chester came to work a couple of days later and he thanked us for dragging him from the bar. He said, "You know, I woke up in the back seat of that old car, and thought somebody had stolen the whole steering wheel and dash. The next thing I knew, a buddy of mine (Jim Masters) was driving the car, he said, "We're going to a bar in Dayton. I hardly remember being at the bar in Dayton, but I remember two women. An old one and a young one. I think they might have been mother and daughter. The bar was next door to a small motel and we intended to take those women to our rooms.

"My buddy, he left with the young one, but I just couldn't bring myself to invite that old one to my room. At least I thought I couldn't. The next thing I knew, I was in bed with her, staring right into her face. The first thing I thought was, *Where am I? And who in the hell is this?* She looked to be at least eighty years old. I turned over and there were her false teeth soaking in a glass of water. I eased out of bed as quietly as I could. I didn't want to wake her. I just wanted to get the hell out of there.

"I thought I was home free. I was almost to the door, tucking my shirt in as I went. She woke up, yawned and said, 'Where are you going, Hon?' I said, "Oh, I'm just going up the street to get us a six-pack. I'll be back in a few minutes." She said, in an oh so sexy voice, 'I'll be right here waiting for you.' 'For whatever the reason, I was blaming it all on Masters. He's not a big guy so I decided to beat the tar out of him. I didn't know the little son of a bitch had been in the Marines.

"I kicked his door open and said, 'You son of a bitch. You let me go to bed with that old hag. I'm going to break your neck.' I made a grab for that little guy, and he took me by the arm, and he threw me down a long hallway. When I got to the other end of that hallway, he was there waiting for me. He grabbed me again and threw me back toward the other end. I just couldn't believe what was happening. I couldn't touch the guy. I thought I was surrounded.

"So, I told him, you caught me drunk. I went to my room and made a pot of coffee. I drank that pot of coffee and smoked half of a pack of cigarettes. I was bold, sober, and mad again. I went back, and kicked his door open again and yelled, 'I'm back,' and he did it again.

"You know, I had a decent life going for me. I was working at William Bailey Manufacturing. I had a home, a pretty wife and two daughters. I just couldn't leave the bottle alone. I used to call her from the jailhouse. I would say, 'Honey!' And she would say, 'In Jail again.' And I would say, 'By God, I am too. What did they get you for?' I was too drunk to know I was divorced till someone threw me out of the house."

And then, there was Bill Dunbar. He had drifted into town about twenty years before. He was a broom maker by trade, which was a skilled trade, but a hobo trade. He was originally from Terre Haute Indiana. Like Charlie Ballenger, he didn't know much about his past, nor how old he was. Truthfully, I think the man had spent a large portion of his life in a drunken stupor. He was a small fellow. He was short and skinny. It looked as if the flesh has shriveled and shrunk over his bones. He lived in a boarding house on the other side of the railroad tracks, just a couple of hundred yards from Vining.

Walking home one day, I heard a loud argument between what sounded like a man and a woman. As I got closer, I realized the sound was coming from the upstairs window of the boarding house where Bill lived. Then I saw Bill's clothes flying through the open window. As I passed, I saw Bill following the woman each time she took another load to the window. He was begging her for another chance, and she wasn't having it. He kept saying, "Now, Judy, you know I'll pay you."

And she said, "That's what you said the last time, mister. Now get out."

Just then Chester pulled in with his Buick, and said, "Looks like Dunbar's getting kicked out again. Help me out, Wynn. We'll put his stuff in my car for now." Bill continued to plead with the woman as we packed his things into Chester's car. There were a lot of clothes, a small stereo, a folding chair, and a small folding table when things stopped flying from the window. Chester had just enough room left in the car to get in and drive away.

No one saw nor heard from Bill Dunbar for more than two weeks. In the meantime, Chester had his own problems, and he's still squeezing in and out of his car. I guess he got tired of hauling Bill's stuff around. He stopped at the at the corner of Columbus Avenue and Burnett Road. He got out the folding table and the folding chair. He put Bill's things on display and had a rummage sale. When it was over, he had sold or given away everything Bill Dunbar owned.

Bill showed up a couple of days later. He pretended not to be upset with Chester, but anyone could see that he was. He told Chester he had a couple of bottles of wine and asked if they could go for a drive in Chester's car. I was standing with Roy Kelly when he called

Chester over and said to him, "Chester. You'd better watch that little son of a bitch. He's dangerous. He told Walter Wells he was going to hit you in the head with a wine bottle."

Chester replied, "Who? Little Dunbar? If he messes with me, I'll slap the piss out of him."

The two of them got into Chester's car and headed east on Columbus Avenue. They were at Reed Park sitting at a picnic table when, without warning, Bill swung a wine bottle. Chester saw it coming, but not in time. Chester tried to lean back, but the thick portion of the bottom of the bottle struck him at the top of his forehead. Chester was knocked out cold.

Bill took Chester's car and left him on the ground with a fractured skull. Bill stopped at a southside bar called Jim's place, where he picked up a passenger. No one heard anything from him till the next morning. The Green County Sheriff called Vining asking for information about Bill Dunbar. He had lost control of Chester's car on a country road near Xenia. The passenger he had picked up at Jim's place was dead. Bill had been arrested and was being charged with vehicular homicide. He told police, he didn't remember hitting Chester. He also said the man who was killed should have known better than to crawl into a car with a drunk driver.

Bill Dunbar was sentenced to three years in a minimum-security prison in Chillicothe.

As strange as it might seem, Chester said he missed Bill Dunbar. After all, I guess they were birds of a feather. Shortly after that, Chester George was walking from his apartment to his car when he collapsed. He was rushed to Mercy Hospital in Springfield where he was given open-heart surgery. Chester George died on the operating table. He was only forty-three years old.

Chapter Twenty-One

It's strange how the face of the world can change so dramatically with the seasons. The greens of summer, the autumn colors, and the bright sunny days are gone. You step out one day and the world is brown and drab. To make things worse, it's dark when you go to work, and dark when you go home. It's depressing no matter who you are. There are a few things you can do to compensate for the loss of sunlight. But you must look for outdoor activities.

On a late Sunday afternoon, my brother-in-law (Bill Skiles) invited us all to go for a ride. So, the five of us piled into his Mercury Marquis and headed out. It was mid-November 1971. We drove north on Burnett Road, then east on Columbus Avenue. Bill drove slowly as we passed through Reed Park. We crossed the old steel bridge and the spot where Clarkie and I spent a Friday afternoon a month or so before. We passed an area of the park that I had not yet seen. There were crabapple trees and large sycamore trees along what looked to be man-made lakes. Bill said the lakes had once been the city's water supply. There was a song playing on Bill's car radio. It was called 'Imagine' by John Lennon. I thought to myself, *Boy, that song can really make you think.*

Bill turned east again, up a hill and into a construction area where a reservoir was being built. It was called the Clarence J Brown Reservoir, in honor of a man who had been Ohio's Lieutenant Governor. Brown had also represented Ohio in the United States House of Representatives. Bill drove to the top of the hill and parked the car. We all took a walk along the top of what was becoming the wall of the dam. We were looking out over fields and woods that would soon be under water. This was the dam Clarkie had told me about. There was Buck Creek, still undisturbed, and still winding through it all. The creek flowed directly below us through the new spillway.

There was a lot to think about that day. Lily and Bill were full of excitement. They had just found out they were going to have a baby. They were also looking for another place to live. Bill worked on the west side of town, and they wanted a place on the ground floor with no stairs. They had always wanted a child and they were going to take every precaution during her pregnancy. Ernie and Judy – they were missing home. They were planning to move back to Kentucky. They were not sure just when, but it would happen sooner, than later.

Gasoline was 23 cents per gallon. It would take ten dollars' worth to make the trip to Weeksbury and back. So, we all chipped in and went home for a visit during the Thanksgiving break. Not much changes in Weeksbury. Lily joined my mother in cooking the Thanksgiving feast, and we watched the Macy's parade on TV, followed by college football.

The Saturday of that weekend my brother Jimmy and I visited Collier Rock. I borrowed a camera to get some pictures. I wanted to show the folks in Ohio where I had come from. It was unseasonably warm and dry that day and there was little or no wind. The leaves had fallen but there were still some beautiful autumn colors. There were evergreen trees scattered over the mountains and some trees that had not yet dropped their leaves. All those colors were visible for about a mile. Further on, the mountain colors became blue, then purple. Just like the words of the Irving Berlin song.

There's something invigorating about standing on a lofty perch like Collier Rock. You feel as if you're the only one there. No one could be this high, this adventurous. You feel as if the entire world must look up to you. But then you venture down from your perch and realize just how small and insignificant you really are.

There was not a lot of conversation that Sunday as we returned to Springfield. I think we were all a little homesick. We all returned to work on Monday and back into the routine. By the end of the day on Tuesday, the homesickness had passed.

Vining had another building just across the railroad track which they referred to as the warehouse. The building was about ten thousand square feet and housed truck-loads of finished goods waiting to be shipped. On the very next day, a water main broke under Columbus Avenue just up the street from the warehouse. The break occurred in the wee hours of the morning, and before it was discovered, Vining's warehouse had three feet of standing water. Truck-loads of finished goods were thought to have been ruined, but the Leventhal brothers were smarter than that.

The main plant where I worked had a room which we called the dry-house. It was a room about sixteen feet wide and forty feet long. The temperature inside that room was kept at one hundred and forty degrees, where brooms were dried as a part of the process. The finished goods would be brought from the warehouse back to the main plant. All the packaging would have to be removed. The brooms would have to go through the scraping process again, then placed in the dry-house for eight hours, repackaged and shipped back to the warehouse.

All this had to be done without interrupting regular production. This created endless amounts of overtime. The key players in all this were myself, Ernie, Frankie Fugate, and Roy Kelly. We worked seven days a week for three full weeks and as much as sixteen hours a day. I thought it was a great opportunity. All that extra money, and at Christmas time. I was even doing math in my head, but my heart fell to my feet when I looked at my paycheck. Most of it had been taken for taxes.

Vining was a noisy place until you got used to it. But after a while you hardly noticed it until lunchtime when most of the machinery was shut down. It's still interesting to me today, the many stages and processes the raw materials passed through to become a finished product. It started in the rear of the production area, where about ten to fifteen women worked. There were long vibrating tables where broom corn was sorted and arranged into different grades.

I still remember their faces, but I really wish I could remember the names of those women. Nepotism was never an issue with Vining's workforce. In fact, it might even have been embraced. Mothers and fathers worked there, their children, and the husbands and wives of their children. In some cases, there were as many as three generations working at Vining. There was Roy and Kathryn Kelley, their son Roy Junior, his wife Doris, and their son Steve. Frank Fugate, his son Frankie, and his son Dennis. John Gates, his wife Marilyn, and their daughter Pat. John Gates also had a sister who worked there. Her name was Margret Coons. John and Loudine Johnson, their two daughters, and their husbands. There were others, but you get the picture. I had one relative working there, and he was leaving.

The change happened sooner than I had expected. Lily and Bill moved to 320 North Jackson Street, on the west side of town. Not long after that, Ernie and Judy moved back to Kentucky. That made the world around me seem even more strange and confusing.

I forgot to mention that Frank Fugate had two brothers who worked at Vining. The first was Martin, who was bald, a Santa Clause looking fellow. He was a pleasant fellow, quick with a joke and fun to work with. Then there was Thurman.

Thurman fought through some terrible times in Europe during the Second World War. He had some terrible times afterwards as well. He had a son who was an excellent baseball player, his name was Larry. The New York Yankees had a farm club at Cooper Stadium in Columbus. One day, Larry went to Columbus and tried out for the Yankees. The agents were interested. Thurman knew that for some reason Larry was not playing at his best. Soon after, it was discovered that Larry had leukemia. That family fought that for years, but Larry died at the age of thirty-two. Larry's death may or may not have been the reason, but Thurman's wife died not long after that, leaving him alone in the world.

I began to look more closely, at my co-workers. Some of them had been working there since the Leventhal family purchased the business in the early 1930s. Some came after the Second World War, some after Korea. Now a group from Vietnam who would be here after the next war. As people and families, they were different, but in so many ways they were all the same. They were unable to dream beyond a factory worker's paycheck. They did the same laborious, monotonous tasks each day, five to six days per week as the years passed. They collected their pay, paid their bills, and counted their change; which was also gone before the next paycheck. As their children finished high school, they too became a spoke in the same wheel. I watched as people got old before their time. They all seemed to be smokers, and at the end of the day, their cars were parked in front of the local taverns.

Sitting here now, some of those ladies and their names came back to me. There was Pauline Rose, Nina Talbert, Erma Nelson, Pat Engel, Marilyn Gates, Lilian Hawkins, Kathryn Kelly, and Margret Coons. There were others, but those are the names I remember.

One day at the end of my shift, I walked past Margret Coons, and I jokingly said to her, "Margret! Why don't you get on out of here for the day? It'll all be here tomorrow."

She said, "The only way to get out of this place, is to die out of it." I just passed the comment off as coming from someone who had worked through thirty years of repetition.

I was in the restroom washing my hands when I heard loud voices, and people rushing through the plant. I rushed out and headed to a circle of people. I heard Bob Stapleton say, "It's too late." Margret was laying on her back with one leg folded under her. Her gaze was straight ahead, her eyes dim. Margret suffered a massive heart attack and was probably dead before she hit the floor. An ambulance came and took her body away.

Everyone soon began to drift away except John Gates, who was her brother. He was sitting at the front dock, as if perhaps in shock. Then he began to weep uncontrollably. John said, "You know, I've worked here almost forty years. I've seen a lot of people come and go, but that's the first time I've ever seen someone die in here. And why did it have to be my sister? She was only forty-eight years old."

Chapter Twenty-Two

I kept thinking about that day, and what Margret's family must have been going through. And I thought about myself, and what the future held for me. I had always dreamed of travel and adventure. But I had to find a way of getting a better education. How much of a future was there for a high school dropout? One day, during my lunch break, I went to the pay-phone at the front dock. A phone book hung beneath it. I nervously searched the yellow pages, then dialed 323-4249. It rang twice and a friendly voice on the other end said, "US Marines, Sergeant Dawson." Monday of the next week, I took a preliminary test at the recruiter's office and was shocked when he said I passed. Thursday of the same week I was taken along with eight other guys to Columbus, where we spent an entire day taking a written exam. I was even more surprised to learn that I had passed those tests as well.

We were taken to the same building the following Thursday and given a physical exam. I was not surprised to have passed that one. There must have been a hundred or more of us who were sworn in to active duty, but only a few were bound for the Marine Corps. We were taken to the Columbus Airport. From there we were flown to Atlanta, then to Charleston South Carolina. I had never been on an airplane before. I had a window seat on the flight to Atlanta. There were two older but wealthy looking ladies sitting next to me. They were downing cocktail, smoking cigarettes and having the time of their lives. They certainly didn't appear to be uneasy. I looked around at the other passengers, they were reading, laughing and talking. No one appeared to be uneasy, so I felt at ease as well.

We were met in Charleston by a liaison officer, who we thought was rude, to say the least. Recruits had been assembled there from throughout the eastern United States. We were directed to a bus just outside the terminal. We were on our way to Parris Island, South Carolina to begin thirteen weeks of boot camp. It was probably because I was used to winter in Ohio, but it was miserably hot on that bus. Everyone was sweating, the windows were steamed up and you could not see anything along that road. I didn't hear the question, but I heard the driver say, "No, you may not put a window down." Guys were happy on that bus, it was almost like going home on a high school bus after your team just won a huge victory.

I was near the center of the bus, but I saw in the headlights a sign that read U S Highway 17 South. The next sign read, Welcome to Beaufort. The bus stopped at the only red light in town, then turned left onto a narrow causeway. I won't bore the world with more war stories. But boot camp at Parris Island in those days was, as they say, "A trip." Especially for a dumb kid who had no idea what to expect. No one in my family had served in the military since my cousin Johnny in the forties and fifties. I hadn't heard as much as a rumor about what to expect.

The brakes squeaked again. I saw a Marine at the front gate in a sharp uniform step to the driver's open window. The driver mumbled some sort of code. The man stepped back and said, "Very Well. Carry on." After a very short drive, the bus stopped again. A drill instructor stepped up onto the bus, at the same time the rear door opened. The drill instructor said, "There are yellow footprints painted on the deck out here. You maggots have got less than a heartbeat to get off this bus and on those prints."

Someone giggled, and the drill instructor grabbed the man in the front seat and threw him from the bus. The man landed on his hands and knees on the asphalt surface. At that same instant, a drill instructor did the same to a man in the back seat. We all got the message after that. We were pushing, shoving, stumbling and falling to get to those yellow footprints.

We had gone from being miserably hot into a sea-breeze that chilled us to the bone. We were told to stand at attention and told not to move a muscle. As hard as we tried, we all began to shiver, and those who were caught were slapped and punched. In the meantime, a drill instructor walked back and forth in front of what we now knew to be a formation. There were drill instructors all around the formation, but only the man in front was giving instructions.

After about two hours he finally said the words we all wanted to hear. He said, "You're going to march in single file into this building. You're going to be given a number as you enter. You must remember that number for the rest of your life. When you get inside this building you will find a rack with that number on it. You'll find sheets and a blanket. Put those sheets and blankets on that rack in some manner or fashion. Don't bother to make it pretty, for you're not going to be there for long." My number happened to be 38.

He was right. It was still dark outside when we began to hear drill instructors yelling commands and the sound of boot heels on the pavement. I don't think anyone had closed their eyes when drill instructors stormed in, turning over racks and shoving men down the steps. We found ourselves once again on the yellow footprints. A drill instructor said, "I'm going to take you ladies to chow, now I want you to face to your right." There was a large group of us, I'm not sure how many, but someone turned to the left. I heard a thud, and drill instructors screaming at him, I'm not even sure what they were saying to the man.

The drill instructor then said, "Now when I give you the word, you will step off with your left foot." When the command was given, a man stepped off with his right foot and endured the same treatment. We entered the chow-hall still in civilian clothes. We were screamed at, scoffed at, and ridiculed by anyone who had been there one week longer than we had. We were taught to keep our head and eyes straight ahead and our mouths shut.

After breakfast, we were taken to a room with a row of chairs and older black men with clippers. Each man's hair was peeled to the scalp in seconds. We were told to strip and place all our clothes and personal belongings into a bag. Then we were herded into a room with more footprints. Suddenly, ice cold water poured from showerheads directly above each person. Those who screamed or tried to flee were beaten. But soon the water became warm, and we knew from that time on what to expect each time we showered.

The rest of the day was spent being measured and fitted for uniforms. We were instructed to dress in what would be our work uniforms. Dress uniforms would not be seen or worn for a long time. We were then marched to a building where a sign over the door read, Forming. Inside that building were rows of long heavy tables. We were instructed to form lines between those tables, with our stomachs touching the man's back in front of us. When the lines were formed, drill instructors stood in front of each line. In unison, they gave a mighty backward shove on each line causing a domino effect. The man in front of me fell between my legs and I fell between the legs of the man behind me and so on. We were told to sit motionless and not make a sound. Drill instructors walked slowly back and forth on the tables to make sure of it.

The only break from this was when we were taken to the mess hall, or at night after the bugler sounded taps. Circulation was always a problem, but you didn't dare twist, squirm, or try to readjust. It was nearly impossible to keep from falling asleep, you had to fight it without moving.

Mid-afternoon on the third day, I didn't think I could take it anymore. I was falling asleep and I couldn't stop it. Just then there was a loud crack. A flashlight struck the back of the head of the man in front of me. He was a muscular black man from New York, by the name Ellerbe. Ellerbe jumped to his feet with both fists clenched. The drill instructor, who was also black, said, "Come on you, street nigger." Ellerbe glared at the drill instructor for a second, then sat back down. I had no problem staying awake after that. We went through nine full days of that. What we didn't know was that we were waiting for enough recruits to arrive to form a company size unit, then and only then would regular training begin.

After nine days in forming we were taken to our squad bay, where we met the three drill instructors who would be with us for the next three months. One of them was the man who had thrown the flashlight. One had been a helicopter crew chief. The senior drill instructor was a large black staff sergeant, who was a veteran of the 1965 Danang landing in Vietnam. His name was Staff Sergeant Campbell. After a lengthy speech, he promised to be fair with us, but he would accept nothing less than one hundred percent.

Our first attempt at drill would be on the way to evening chow. When everyone failed to fall right into step and begin marching, he gave the command to halt, then he said, "Begin." Someone knew this meant to begin an exercise known as bends and thrusts, so the rest of us joined in. The next command was mountain climbers, then leg lifts, then pushups. When you have sat motionless on your butt, on concrete, for nine days, things begin to shut down. These drill instructors were killing us. He finally yelled, "Platoon halt," and everyone jumped to their feet at attention and we were marched on to chow.

During chow, we sat on benches looking straight ahead. Those were the only places to sit on the island, except at night when you were given fifteen minutes to sit on your footlocker and write one letter. The rest of your time was spent in physical training and drill. No one walked anywhere. If you were not in formation marching, then you were running, or as it's called double timing. Any mistake would get you beaten, or exercised to the point of dropping. Worst of all was the humiliation. They stopped at nothing to degrade and dishearten you. Every effort was used to try and break you.

The day would begin at 05:00 with reveille. We were given two minutes to dress, then marched to chow. After that, the day would begin. There was a short break for the noontime meal, another for evening chow, and back to the squad bay at 19:00 hours. We were given five minutes in the shower, then one hour to break down, clean and reassemble of our M-14 service rifles. The last hour was spent shining boots and brass. If there was time, letters were written, then lights out at 21:00 hours.

Two recruits were chosen to walk fire-watch duty. It was a four-hour shift, beginning at 21:00. Your relief would take over at 01:00, and wake up the drill instructor at 05:00 who slept in a separate room. The wake-up call was three loud, open-handed slaps on the door, and a resounding, "Sir, the time on deck is zero, five hundred." I remember being on fire-watch duty one night. I walked along the walls of the squad bay and I just couldn't figure it out. I wasn't drafted. I had volunteered. So, why was I being treated this way? I could see the lights of the mainland, and the only red light in Beaufort. I watched that light change and saw the headlights pass under it. Folks were going their way, totally oblivious to what was going on here on Parris Island, just a few miles away.

But there was no break from the drill instructors, not even at night. It was no surprise to have one of them sneak in and whack someone for snoring, or even breathing too loud. The only way off the island was the causeway. We were warned to stay away from the swamps surrounding the island. It was known for its reptiles, including alligators.

I was chosen for guard duty one night. The purpose for this was to ensure no one tried to make an escape. Remembering the reptiles of Kentucky, I realized this was for the safety of the recruits. My post was about a quarter mile square. I walked a quarter of a mile, turned right, another quarter mile, turned right and so on. That too was a four-hour shift, and I went on duty at 01:00. I was on my second trip around when I met a recruit walking directly toward me, at a fast but awkward pace. His arms and hands dangled loosely at his side and he appeared to be saying something, but there was no sound.

I said in a low voice, "Halt." He didn't seem to hear so I said, "Stop, fool!" He was walking right past me, so

I grabbed his arm. That's when I realized he was sound asleep. He woke up confused, looking around wildly as if to try to figure out where he was. I tried to keep him quiet and find out what building he belonged in. However, the sergeant of the guard came flying over in a jeep. He jumped out and grabbed the man and took him away. Near the end of that shift, the rain started to pour. The sergeant of the guard came by again. He didn't stop the jeep or say anything. He just threw a poncho in my direction and kept moving. That place was everything I imagined a POW camp to be, and then it occurred to me – that's exactly what it was. They were preparing us for that and they were preparing for war.

First phase was three weeks long, and just before we were to start second phase, we were taken to the base chapel. I didn't much care why we were there, it just felt good to sit in a chair. After we had been there about ten minutes, a drill instructor with the rank of gunnery sergeant walked to the altar. He said, "A man is coming out here to speak to you. He fought in Korea and he has served two tours of duty in Vietnam. He is your battalion commander. You will render onto him all the respect you would render onto God." Then he called us to attention.

There were at least seven hundred of us and there was nothing more than a swoosh and we were on our feet, silent and motionless. The man walked to the altar in a Marine Corps dress blue uniform, with lots of shiny badges and ribbons. In a calm voice he said, "Please be seated.

"My name is Lieutenant Colonel Curd. By now you're wondering why you're being treated this way. You're under a lot of pressure. This is only one-third of the pressure you'll feel in combat. You are going through a weeding out process. If you have any weakness, we can send you home from here. We can't always make that promise after you become Marines. It's a proven fact, not everyone is able to make it through Marine Corps boot camp. You can quit now and be transferred to another branch of the military to serve out your term. If you complete this training, you will become a member of the greatest fighting force the world has ever known. If you complete this training, then and only then, will you be permitted to wear our coveted Marine Corps emblem.

"It's not for everyone. We have already shipped out sixty-two recruits from the battalion you are training with, and there will be many more. The completion rate is about fifty-two percent. When you become Marines, the mental testing will decrease but the physical training will increase. The training will never stop as long as you wear that uniform. You'll fight to stay awake in stuffy classrooms, and you'll run till you drop. That is what makes us different from the rest. I hope you didn't think it would be easy."

Chapter Twenty-Three

It was all different after that. Each one of us developed that "You're not going to break me" attitude. But the training got tougher and guys continued to disappear. There were eighty-five of us in my platoon when the training began, but there was only forty-two of us who graduated and left Parris Island wearing the emblem.

It was easy for me when I realized that everything, I did was my own personal struggle. I considered it to be a game, and the trick was to stay one step ahead of it. I went to Kentucky for ten days leave. Then I went to Camp Lejeune, North Carolina to begin an eight-week course called FSTU, or Field Skills Training Unit. I checked in at the Eighth Marine Regiment, then headed to downtown Jacksonville to see what the town adjacent to the base was like. The main drag was Court Street. I honestly thought it was a circus, or a carnival. There was loud music everywhere, neon lights and celebration. People were drunk in the street, and there were rows of drinking establishments. I walked into a place called The Sky Room. It was on the second of a two-story building. It had large windows overlooking Court Street. It was not quite dark outside, but the girls working there were already topless. I thought I had simply stumbled into the wrong place, but no. That was a way of life around large military bases. Drinking and prostitution were rampant. And they were not professional prostitutes. They were the wives and girlfriends of servicemen who were deployed.

There was a sergeant by the name Davis who worked at base supply. I was told that Davis arrived home unexpectedly and found a man on top of his wife. Davis, who had already been tipped off about his unfaithful wife, was armed with a 12-gauge shotgun. He placed the barrel of the gun near the man's rectum and pulled the trigger. The man was a fellow Marine who died instantly. Davis simply told authorities, he thought the man was raping his wife and no charges were ever filed.

There was the case of Chuck and Glenda Carman. There was about a mile of Eighth Marine Regiment that ran along US Highway 17. On the other side of the road was a large military supply store called Saigon Sam's. For decades that business thrived on goods that were stolen from the base. Sadly, it was Marines stealing from Marines. Helmets, canteens, tents, war belts, and all manner of field gear, which we called duce gear.

Even weapons were sold there. And if your gear was stolen, you were told to go to Saigon Sam's to buy back whatever was stolen from you. It was as openly corrupt as the day is long. The owner of Saigon Sam's had a brother who owned a large nightclub next door called Dobbie's Place. Stolen goods were sold at Saigon Sam's and the proceeds were spent at Dobbie's.

Dobbie's never sold as much as a tavern pizza for food. It was all alcohol, and there were at least thirty girls working there. It was a smaller version of Hefner's Playboy club, but maybe a little more hardcore. The Marines loved it. There was no way of knowing how wild the party would become. If things got out of hand, the lucky ones were thrown out before they got hurt. There were brawls and back-room sex. Every day there was a different set of tall tales about the place.

Chuck Carman was serving thirty days of night mess duty. He kept saying he wanted to go there just once for the experience. But while he was working, everyone else was at the party. His buddies kept discouraging him: for two reasons. One was that he was married, the other reason was because Carman's wife was one of the girls.

It had to happen. One evening he walked in and there was his wife. She was topless and holding a serving tray in her hands. What hurt him most is that she pretended not to know him. He made a scene and the bouncers threw him out. Carman walked to the back of the building, sat down on the steps and began to weep. His wife stormed out of the building, jumped into their Pinto station wagon and sped away. They had only been married for a couple of months, and I don't know what happened after that. I never saw Carman again.

It was a little bit like college, except these frats were trained to kill. There was this big, dumb, blond-headed kid; no one could pronounce his name, so we just called him Swede. Before joining the Corps, Swede had been a Merchant Marine. He thought he was the toughest man on the planet, and he probably was. I don't know what his enemies looked like after a fight, but the Swede was always cut or stabbed somewhere on his body. He was a regular on Court Street, and the ladies loved him. At least they loved him on the fifteenth and the thirtieth days of the month. Those were paydays. Some of those ladies who loved him belonged to someone else.

We came in from the field one night, and there was Swede leaning on the corner of the barracks, a puddle of blood at his feet. Fortunately, we always had a medical corpsman with us, so he and a couple of sergeants rushed to help Swede. They stretched him out in the grass and applied pressure bandages to the wounds until the ambulance took him away. Swede was gone for a couple of weeks, and when he came back, he was placed on light duty. That was the second time he'd been cut, and the captain told him if it happened again, he'd be court-martialed. There was little or no tolerance for self-inflicted wounds or irresponsible behavior.

There was a large grassy area between the buildings of the base and US 17. Just a few miles south of the Eighth Marine Regiment was the large Marine air base called the New River Air Station. When there was an emergency somewhere in the world, or when we needed choppers for training, they would use the grassy area for a landing zone. If a unit had to be deployed, helicopters would land there and fly that unit to the air base to board transport planes. We sometimes used the grassy area for recreation at the end of the day. After that we'd walk through the main gate, across 17, to a place called the Chateau Madrid. It was a little classier than Dobbie's or the places on Court Street, but not much. The Chateau was a little safer and they closed at 23:00.

We were playing football on a Friday afternoon when Swede came walking past, still wearing bandages on his arms. Someone called to him, "Hey, Swede! Wanna join us for a beer at the Chateau?"

He said, "No, you guys probably won't be going for a while. I'm just going to go over to Dobbie's for a couple, then I have mess duty tonight."

Someone else yelled, "Hey, Swede, you want to take my sewing kit? You're probably going to need to sew something up before the night's over."

Swede didn't respond, nor did he go to Dobbie's. There was a footpath leading through some woods then back on to 17 and north to Jacksonville. There was a large USO club along the way, with wholesome recreation. But most guys taking the path through the woods were not looking for wholesome activities.

We left the Chateau Madrid at closing time, and near the path through the woods were lots of flashing blue lights. The sentry walking his post heard movement in the bushes and went to investigate. He radioed for help but the sound he heard in the bushes was Swede's final movements. The sentry applied first aid immediately, but it was too late. The Swede bled to death.

I consider myself to be a pretty good judge of character. But characters change under the circumstances we were in. In boot camp, one's old character was broken down or erased altogether. Then a new, stronger, but different character was built.

Lance Corporal Jeffers was a handsome black kid from New Jersey. Looking back, I remember that he looked like Denzel Washington. He was soft-spoken, well-mannered and always willing to help. He was assigned to an M-60 machine gun squad; therefore, his personal weapon was a .45 caliber pistol.

I was on duty one night when the MPs came into the barracks looking for Jeffers. I escorted them to the third deck, where Jeffers was sleeping. It was about 23:00 and the squad bay was dark. One of the MPs held a bright light on Jeffers while the other aimed his sidearm. Jeffers didn't appear to be surprised, but he was not allowed to dress or put on shoes. He was taken away in shorts and a tee shirt.

A couple of hours later I called the MPs and told them I had to make a report, and I needed to know the status on Jeffers. They gave me the number for the Onslow County Sheriff's office. When I called, the man said to me, "You don't have to worry about this one, he's locked safely away. He's being held on suspicion of murder."

The next day Jeffers made a full confession. He had signed out his sidearm at the armory and told them he was going to clean it. He joined up with a friend from another unit. They walked into a convenience store on Lejeune Boulevard and demanded money. The attendant was a man in his early twenties who had gotten out of the service a couple of years before. The irony was that the attendant's father had been killed in a hold up a few years before. When he refused to hand over the money, Jeffers fired two rounds into a potato chip rack. The attendant only laughed. Jeffers put the pistol to the man's head and pulled the trigger. Jeffers parents were shocked; and told the commanding officer that Jeffers had never broken a law in his life until then.

FSTU was a lot of hard work, but it was fun as well. Revile was 05:00 and classes began at 06:00 and ran until the noontime meal. The rest of the day was spent in practical application. Sometimes the day ended at

18:00 hundred hours, sometimes it ended at midnight, depending on the agenda. Unlike boot camp there was some free time or liberty as we called it. Some guys took advantage of every moment of that free time to hit the town. I've seen guys sick, puking and swearing to the good lord above, they would never drink again if they could only make it through the day. But when night rolled around again, they headed off to town.

First names were not used in the military, so I don't know what the guy's first name was. I only knew him as Bullard. He was a handsome black man, and boy did he know it. He openly bragged about his prowess with the ladies. But this prowess kept him out late at night, and he found no sympathy from the senior sergeants who were teaching the courses.

There were stiff penalties for falling asleep in class. The penalty was usually a bucket of cold water. That poor sap got it every day along with anyone sitting close to him. Uniforms had to be clean, pressed and wrinkle-free every day. After that bucket of water was thrown, those who got wet had to spend their break double timing back to the barracks to change. Those sitting close to Bullard got it sometimes twice in a day. Bullard was not the only one who got drenched, but he made the mistake of saying it was because he was black. That only made the penalties worse. Determined to beat the system one day when he just couldn't go on, he hid behind a circle of friends, next to an open window. He leaned against the screen of the open window. He was well hidden from the instructor and was sleeping peacefully. Suddenly a wave of water came through the open window from the outside, drenching him and his entire circle of friends. There was another instructor outside keeping an eye on things.

Until you completed FSTU, you were referred to as skill-less.

The colonel who developed the Field Skills Training Unit's name was Colonel Thorn. He was from West Virginia. He spoke in a loud, high-pitched voice, and he had trouble saying skill-less. It sounded as if he were saying skillet. It was humorous, but everyone taking the course was referred to as a skillet. If a member of the class failed to learn or made the same mistakes, he became the chief skillet. Not an honor you would want bestowed upon you. Three frying pans were tied together and hung from the chief skillet's neck. Wherever the unit marched, the chief skillet walked behind wearing the skillets. Bullard was forced to clonk along behind us through most of the course.

The colonel didn't lie. The training never stopped. Each course took three to eight weeks to complete, and they were all spelled out in initials or acronyms. After the Field Skill Training Unit, there was ITT – Interrogation Translation Team, STANO – Surveillance Target Acquisition and Night Observation. The training became more rigorous and certainly more interesting.

RIP school, or Reconnaissance Indoctrination Phase, consisted of repelling, rope climbing and pre-dawn landings using rubber rafts. RIP school was preparation for jump school at Fort Benning, Georgia. Then there was SPIE rigging. SPIE stood for Special Patrol Insertion and Extraction.

We rappelled from helicopters in four-man teams; the choppers would then fly away. We would then plant our traps, sensors, or whatever the mission called for. We would call for the helicopters to return, they would lower the same rope we used in the drop. Our body harnesses were attached to the rappelling rope, and we were flown back to friendly territory suspended from the rope. My crowning achievement was the completion of the US Armies Special Forces School at Fort Bragg, North Carolina. Although, as Marines, we were not allowed to wear the Green Beret. But that's OK, we had our emblem.

Chapter Twenty-Four

The Marine Corps and the 1970s flew past me like a blur. In 1976, I had married the prettiest girl I had ever seen. Her name was Claudia Jo Riley, everyone called her Jo. She was from Ohio and she had a one-year-old daughter from a failed relationship. I reckon I fell in love with her and her daughter.

Late spring 1978, we were living in a trailer park on Highway 53, just a few miles west of the base. I'm not sure how it is today, but trailers were the only thing available near Lejeune in the 1970s. There was a long wait for base housing and I was never in one place long enough to apply for a house on base.

The park was owned by a retired Marine by the name of Mr Ailshire. Ailshire was a widower who lived alone just across the highway. He was a gruff old man who had been severely injured in the Korean War. The only company he ever had was when someone stopped by to pay rent. But he wasn't exactly lonely. He had a mean old tomcat, a scruffy looking dog, and a large black bird. When someone stopped to pay their rent, the old man wrote out a receipt and the bird did the talking. The bird would look you in the eye, turn its head, call you a wall-banger and say, "Pay the rent and get the hell out." And then the bird would mock the cat and bark like the dog. Then he would say, "Told you to pay the rent and get the hell out." The cat terrorized the dog, and the dog terrorized every dog in the neighborhood. I swear it was like the old man was living in a cartoon.

Military life is tough on married life. I saw it so many times. A young man would be deployed, and his buddy would move in with his wife before the end of the day. The sanctity of marriage was not well respected in those days. There were other infidelities as well. A young lady knocked at our door one night and said, "Someone's in Frank and Nancy's house, and they are gone on leave."

I grabbed a ball bat and as I ran toward the house a black man bolted from the front steps with a white sack in his hand. I yelled, "What are you doing?"

He said, "Hey, man, I'm just picking up some shit." I never stopped running but the man was too far ahead of me. He jumped into a car that was waiting for him and they sped away without turning on the car's lights. Judging from his haircut and his physical abilities I was sure the man was another Marine. What's worse is that he was someone close enough to the victims to know they were gone for a few days.

On a rainy night a few days after that another incident occurred, this one far more tragic. I was on air alert at the base. The Marine Corp is known for rapid response to national emergencies. The air alert force is a vanguard that is packed and ready at a moment's notice. It is a six months duty, and the air alert unit can be picked up anywhere on base. From there the force is taken to New River Air Station on helicopters and flown out on C-130 transport planes. When you are on air alert you are at the base from very early morning till late at night. Sometimes you can't go home.

It had been another long day at the base. We had just had dinner and were just about to go to bed. My wife said to me, "You look worn out. Why don't you go on to bed? I'm going to do the dishes first." I was very tired, so I thought I would take her up on her offer.

I could hear the rain on the roof of the trailer, and I thought, *it's going to be a nice, cool night to sleep.* I sat down on the bed and reached down to untie my boots when I heard a chilling sound out on the main road.

Most drivers will tell you that tires will not squeal on wet pavement. I'm telling you these tires were screaming in the pouring rain. Then I heard a loud crash. I jumped to my feet and headed for the front door. My wife asked where I was going, and I asked her if she had heard the crash. She said, "Yes, but don't worry about it someone will stop." I didn't take the time to grab a jacket. The only things I had on were trousers, boots and a tee shirt. As I reached the bottom of the steps, I heard a scream. When I left the street lights of the park, I realized just how incredibly dark it was. I got to Highway 53 and headed in the direction of the crash. The loudness of the sound led me to believe the crash was closer.

Running up the road I met someone coming toward me with a flashlight. The only thing I could see was a person's feet and a spot on the road just in front of him. A man's voice asked, "Do you know first aid?"

I said, "Yes, I'll do what I can."

He said, "You'd better get on up there." He was an older man. He gave me his light and I ran past him, and I began to see the wreckage.

It was one of those sporty two-door cars. The kind with one long door on either side. A Trans Am or a Firebird. I couldn't believe what I was seeing. The car had left the road and into a grassy ditch that had been mowed but had water running in it. The car traveled along the ditch a hundred feet or so then struck a pine tree that was about two feet in diameter. The car had been cut completely in two, straight across the back floorboard. The front portion of the car remained behind the tree and the rear portion was about fifty feet further on and had been stopped by a driveway and culvert.

The front seat was mangled, and the driver was bent backward over what was left of it. When I got to him I could see that he was just a young man. His body was convulsing. I knew he was dying, but I wasn't ready to give up. There was a great deal of blood on the floorboard and I needed to know where it was coming from. I got on my knees where I could see up under the dash. About a foot below the man's knees, his trousers looked as if they were folded, with no legs in them. I could not see either of his feet. They were crammed into the wreckage. His legs had been severed. The windshield was gone, so I grabbed the rubber seal that was left. My intention was to use it for a tourniquet. But first I had to make sure he was breathing, and he was not.

Another flashlight was now shining on the victim. A woman's voice asked, "Is that you, Wynn?" I recognized her as a lady named Karen who lived in the closest house to the wreck. She had been to our house a couple of times. My wife had purchased Avon products from her.

I grasped the young man's chin with the thumb and fingers of my left hand to open his mouth. I held his nose with the thumb and forefinger of my right hand. His teeth were loose in their sockets, his cheek and jawbone were also crushed. The young man's face felt almost like a balloon filled with water.

Oddly enough I could see a spark of life still left in his eyes. That gave me hope as I started blowing air into his lungs. I didn't see blood in his mouth, but I could taste blood. I continued for a few minutes, then I stopped to see if he was breathing on his own. I was looking into his green eyes and I saw the spark go dim. I knew he was gone, but the rule was to keep going until help arrived.

I heard sirens and saw blue lights coming. The first to arrive was an MP unit from New River. Two MPs came down into the ditch, and one of them said, "Hey, man! That's Cott. I know that dude. Oh my God, man, it's Cott." After that one MP was, as they say, freaking out. The other was trying to console him. The only help I got from them was more light.

Just a couple of minutes later a highway patrol officer arrived. He turned a bright spotlight on the wreckage, then came to help. He shined his flashlight into the young man's face and said to me, "You can stop. There's nothing more you can do." I followed him up onto the driveway where the other portion of the car had come to rest. He asked if I had seen the wreck. I said no. I told him I heard the crash and then what sounded like a woman's scream. He asked if I knew who had screamed and I said no. The crash had occurred directly in front of Karen's house. She walked over just after that question, so I asked her if she knew who had screamed.

Just then we heard someone moaning. The sound was coming from the bushes beyond the driveway, about fifty feet from the wreck. I took Karen's flashlight, and the trooper and I fought our way through the brush where we found a young lady. When the light hit her, she began to scream. Paramedics had just arrived, and they rushed to her immediately.

Then we found another victim. A young man sitting on his backside, directly in the flow of the water. He was obviously in shock. He thought he was still in the back seat of the car. He held a broken and soggy cigarette between his fingers, and asked, "Is anyone going to give me a light back here?" Aside from his confusion, he didn't appear to have a scratch on him.

The young lady was strapped to a stretcher and her only apparent injury was a broken leg. However, when they were taking her to the ambulance, she saw the wreckage and began to scream. She did manage to give an account of what happened. She said that Cott was her boyfriend. They lived in a trailer park called Clear View, about ten miles to the west. The other man had been visiting them. Her boyfriend had an argument with the landlord and was angry. They all jumped into the car and took off. She said Cott was driving, she was in the front seat with him and the other man was in the backseat. She said Cott reached over to turn on the windshield wipers and lost control.

The mystery was, how the young man drove ten miles in the rain without the wipers being on. The rain had been non-stop that day. For that reason, the trooper thought the driver might have been impaired. He asked if I had smelled alcohol on him and I said no. Most of the remaining details were printed in the local newspapers the next day. I didn't learn much more than I already knew, except that all three people in the car were originally from Rhode Island.

I've seen death many times throughout my lifetime. I guess we all see death. But what sticks with me, is the fact that my eyes were just a few inches from his when his soul left him. It was almost as if he wasn't dying, just going somewhere else. I hope you never have to see it, but if you ever do, it will enforce your notion of life after death.

The 1970s were another tumultuous decade. Rock star Jimmy Hendrix died in September 1970 and Janis Joplin died just two weeks later.

Watergate dominated the news, even after President Nixon resigned in August of 1974. Gerald Ford finished out Nixon's term, but then was defeated by Jimmy Carter in 1976.

Elvis Presley died in 1977. Disco music dominated the airwaves.

In 1979, the Pittsburg Steelers defeated the Dallas Cowboys in Super Bowl thirteen. The Pittsburg Pirates defeated the Baltimore Orioles to win the World Series.

On November forth 1979, Iranian militants stormed the US embassy in Tehran, capturing fifty Americans. They were held until Ronald Regan took office in January 1981.

Chapter Twenty-Five

The Marines had become my family. I had furthered my education and accomplished some things I never thought possible for me. I had been sent to many places. Some of them were places I wanted to go to, and some were places I did not. With the years I had spent I should probably have made it a career. But my wife did not like the lifestyle, and I really couldn't blame her. We had little children, and I was gone a lot. Don't get me wrong. She liked the Corps, and we had a lot of friends who were in the same situation. Jo loved the pageantry of the Corps. She would get dressed up and we would go to the Marine Corps Ball. That was a celebration everyone enjoyed every November tenth. (The Marine Corps Birthday.)

I was an infantry sergeant with a platoon. I drilled or marched my platoon as part of everyday training. On Friday mornings the base marching band would come to Eighth Marine Regiment. We would march our troops to the music. My wife would bring the kids to the base to watch as we marched our troops with the band. But she said she would divorce me if I reenlisted. I loved the Corps, but I loved my wife even more.

I left the Marine Corps in the spring of 1980, with the rank of sergeant, and we moved back to Ohio. Things were terrible on the outside. The price of gasoline was out of sight. And starving men who had been laid off from the factories struggled to feed their families. Everyone who had ever helped to trim a tree created a tree removable service. Anyone who had ever helped to nail on a roof created a roofing company. But no one had money to hire these new businesses. The Carter Administration had made a mess of the economy, and the Iranians were still holding American hostages.

Things were not so bad for me, however. I went back to work at Vining with a management position. And because I had worked there before I joined the service, I had nine years of seniority. The working hours had been rearranged in the years I had been gone. We now worked eight and three-quarter hours per day and five hours on Friday for a total of forty. The work-day ended at 11:00 on Friday but I still had lots of energy. The problem I had was working indoors. Vining had what everyone called factory windows. The windows were made of a frosted type glass. Without the florescent lights, inside the plant was never brighter than an overcast day. I longed to make my living outdoors.

The money was great, but I was only twenty-six years old, and I had picked up some other skills along the way. I had grown up helping to build things. In addition to that, I had two brothers-in-law who were in the construction business. One of them was my wife's eldest brother Mike Riley, the other was her elder sister's husband John Hodson. Both of those guys were talented and hard-working contractors. After I married Jo, I worked with those guys for cash every time I came home on leave. I sometimes made more money in a week than I made in a month's military pay.

In the summer of 1980, I wrote my first contract. I rebuilt a rundown garage and made it like new. The owner of the garage worked for a rather large company called Cascade Steel Corporation. He passed the word around to his co-workers and the contracts kept coming. And I was still working forty hours per week at Vining. At a time when the best-paid factory workers were making less than three hundred dollars per week, I was making seven hundred to a thousand.

I no longer worked with John and Mike, for two reasons. John lived almost three hours away near Ashland Kentucky. And Mike. Well that an interesting story in itself. Mike was one of eight children born to Raymond and Janet Riley. Raymond was a handsome man and Janet was a beautiful lady. Their children inherited those good looks. There were three boys who were very handsome, and there were five girls who were very pretty.

Raymond worked for the Ohio highway engineers, but a heart condition took him at forty-five. Mike was the eldest. His story goes back beyond Raymond's death.

The family lived in the rough-tough White Hall neighborhood of Columbus. Mike was, for the lack of better words, a wild one. He ran off and joined the Marine Corps in 1966. But when Uncle Sam found out he was only sixteen, he was sent home before he got through boot camp. In Mike's eyes, this made him feel like a loser. It wasn't long until he had his first scrape with the law. Before the end of the year 1966, he was sent to prison for forgery. By the time I met him in the mid-1970s he had already been in and out of prison for years. He had also developed an addiction to drugs.

Mike was not a tall man, but a very muscular one. I guess he worked out a lot in prison. Mike had light brown, almost blond, hair and blue eyes. He looked like a cross between Mick Jagger and Charles Bronson. He was also very intelligent and fun to hang out with. I wanted to stay on the right side of the law, but I couldn't resist Mike's friendship. He spent a lot of time in prison, but each time he got out he would find me. Despite all his shortcomings, I loved him like a brother. In fact, I loved the entire Riley family as if they were my own.

Mike was a kind and generous man, yet a dangerous and unpredictable one if provoked. But for whatever the reason he respected me, and he was very obedient to me.

Mike would be sent to prison for a couple or three years, then he'd show up again ready to start a new life. But there were demons he just couldn't overcome. We had rented a house from Ralph Jernigan, a good friend and co-worker at Vining. I came home from work one day in March of 1982 and I saw a black plastic bag on top of the refrigerator. I asked my wife if she'd been shopping. She said, "No, Mike's upstairs in bed." I looked in the bag and saw money. I knew in an instant where that money came from.

I had heard that Mike and his younger brother had been on a robbing spree, and now his life of crime had come to our door. I raced up those stairs and jumped on top of Mike. I slapped him as hard as I could on both sides of his face and he showed no response what so ever. I knew I would have to allow him to sleep it off. Whatever he was taking had him completely anesthetized.

He didn't as much as move for about fourteen hours. Every minute of which, I was sure the police would be knocking at the door. He was still groggy and needed more time to wake up, but I had no chivalry for him. I told him to take his belongings, get out, and never come back until he got his act together.

Mike showed up a couple of days later with his long-time girlfriend Sandy. They promised to behave if we would let them stay with us for a couple of days. I just couldn't find a way to say no. However, I gave them some conditions. There would be no drugs and no fighting among themselves. Furthermore, if the police came for them, they would not resist. They also had to be willing to swear that Jo and I had nothing to do with any of their crimes.

Two nights later they had their first fight. Mike was outside, reaching in, swinging his fist blindly at Sandy. She was inside, with Mike's arm pinned in the door. My children were scared to death. I jumped up from my chair, told them to shut up, stop that racket and go to bed. They stopped instantly, but not before Mike stepped out to the street to break the windshield of Sandy's car. After that they went quietly to bed.

They disappeared again after that, but that weekend there was a knock at the door. I opened it to a large black man who called me by name and said he was looking for Mike. I said, "Oh, yeah, what for?"

He said, "Don't get me wrong. Mike's my friend. We grew up together in White Hall. We've even done time together." He told me his name but said everyone called him Moon.

I said, "Well, listen. It's a little late and my wife and kids are asleep. Why don't you just have a seat here on the porch and I'll get us a beer."

I don't think I have ever talked to a nicer guy. And boy did he tell some stories of him and Mike. He also told me he had been a stand-in for a movie. I was enthralled, but he said it was no big deal. It was a Robert Redford movie called Brubaker. It was a movie about a prison, and it was filmed near Chillicothe Ohio. It was the final scene where about a thousand people stood along a prison fence and clapped for Robert Redford. He said he was paid twenty-five dollars for his part. He seemed to think Mike would show up, so we talked for about two hours. I kept thinking *"This young man could have been somebody. But what kind of future is he going to have?"* My intuition was right. I watched him drive away and I got the sad, sinking feeling that I would never see him again. Moon was shot and killed in a drug deal the very next weekend.

Johnny Riley was Mike's younger brother. Not to be confused with John Hodson the brother-in-law who was a contractor. Johnny Riley was married to a lovely woman named Teri and they had three children. Johnny spent three years in the army. He got out in the early 1970s and went to work for Cardinal Vending. He had worked for them until Mike was released from prison. But then he became a part of Mike's crime spree.

My wife's mother Janet came to visit for a while that spring. She had remarried, and things didn't seem to be going well for her. Her new husband was an OK guy, but very controlling. They lived near Ashland, about three hours away. I think she just needed a little time away from him.

Her visit began on Easter weekend 1982. On Easter Sunday we had a picnic at John Brian State Park, a few miles south of Springfield. The children played until they wore themselves out. It was such a perfect day. One of those days you hoped would never end. When we got home our children, Nikki and Jeremy, went straight to bed. Jo, Janet and I sat in the backyard talking till almost midnight.

Things quickly changed the next day when I went to work. Ralph Jernigan walked over to me and said. "Boy, those old Riley boys are in for it now."

I said, "What are you talking about, Ralph?"

He said, "They were on every news channel in Columbus last night. They led the police on a high-speed chase for over three hours before they caught up with them. But they're in jail now."

Mike and Johnny had gone into the business of robbing drugstores. They had robbed every drugstore they could find between Columbus Ohio and Ashland Kentucky. They carried guns, and Mike's weapon of choice was a sawed-off 12-gauge shotgun. They had a routine. They would bolt through the front door of a drugstore and Mike would blast the security cameras off the wall. Needless to say, they had everyone's attention after that point. They robbed a drugstore called The Little Darby in West Jefferson Ohio. They found it to have been an easy target, so they went back a couple of weeks later. But the folks at the store saw them coming and hit the alarm. They robbed the place and were just pulling out of the parking lot when they saw the police coming. That's when the chase began that ended their spree.

I went home immediately and knocked at Janet's bedroom door. I said, "Janet, could you get up please. We need to talk." The door flew open and she had a look of horror on her face.

She asked, "Wynn, are my boys dead?"

I said, "No, Janet, but I'm afraid they're in a lot of trouble."

Johnny Riley had never been in trouble, so he was only given a sentence of three years with probation. Mike was sentenced to ten years. I lost track of the two of them after that, but I didn't stop thinking about them.

Chapter Twenty-Six

The owners of Vining (Fred and Harry Leventhal), had made generous contributions to hospitals and schools in the area. Therefore, they had a lot of influence. I was asked if I would like to attend night classes at Wright State University, and I accepted. The classes were only two nights per week in business administration. It didn't cost me anything and I don't think it cost the Leventhal's anything either.

My father passed away on the first full day of summer in 1983. I had three weeks paid vacation on the books at Vining, and I took it. My father's last request was not to let it rain on his grave. He had described what he wanted, and I built it. It was so strange that seconds after the last shingle was nailed on, it rained hard for just a few minutes.

I then took my family to Austin Texas to visit my wife's relatives who had moved there a few years before. We had fun. Every day was beer, food, and volleyball in the pool. But then, I became extremely restless. I wanted to get back to work. I had never gone that long without working in my life.

Working for Vining had several benefits. It was more than a steady paycheck. It provided healthcare and a retirement plan. Vining had plenty of young men just like me who had lots of energy at the end of the week, and families to support. Those young men became the workforce for my contracting business. We replaced roofs, installed siding and windows, built patio decks, fences and barns.

I didn't want to buy a house, I wanted to find the right spot and build my own. In late summer 1983, I thought I had found it. It was three acres on Collins Arbogast Road in South Vienna, twelve miles east of Springfield. It was on a knoll that stood above the miles of farmland that surrounded it. It had enough large hickory trees to shade the entire lot. It had the cutest little dwelling on it, called a cedar chalet. It was an A-frame type construction, built on a mobile home chassis. It looked like a gingerbread house. It had a living room, bathroom, kitchen, and a spiral stairway leading to a bedroom in the loft. It had large windows, and each window had a flower box with flowers growing in them.

I heard about the place from Bob Buck. He was a co-worker at Vining and a member of my workforce. The property had belonged to his wife's mother, who had lived there alone until her death earlier that year. In fact, she was all alone there when the worst blizzard in a hundred years struck in 1978. The national guard rescued her with a helicopter.

I had found my utopia. It was a time in my life when I was trying to erase the temperament of the Marine Corps and readjust to civilian life. There were times when I just needed to be alone. I would go out to that property, make a small fire and gaze out at the fields and the sky. There was a splendid view of the moonrise and the sunset. I was a smoker then and a coffee drinker. I spent hours there doing both, just dreaming, and daydreaming. Although I was not much for pipe dreams. I was a doer. And the first thing I needed to do was move the gingerbread house out of the way, so I could build my house. I had it moved further back on the property, reinstalled the utilities and rented to a Bachler friend by the name Bob Brown. Then I hired a man with a backhoe to dig a foundation for our new home.

The problem was, I couldn't get my wife interested. She said, "I'm not living out there in the sticks." But that wasn't the only problem I was having with my marriage. The first year had been great, but our marriage had gone downhill ever since. I loved Jo dearly, and we had two beautiful children, but I couldn't find a way to make her happy. I certainly can't place all the blame on her. I was working and going to school. I guess I was looking too far ahead to realize that my home-life was falling apart.

We separated in the spring of 1984, and the divorce was final that fall. She moved in with a younger guy who had been one of my troops in the Marine Corps. He had visited us a couple of times before he got out in 1982. I had suspected there might have been something between them, but I didn't think I could stop it. We both knew a divorce was coming, but we had agreed that whatever happened, the children would be kept together.

She was given custody of the children, and the first thing she did was drop our daughter at her mother's home two hours to the south. She took our son to her boyfriend's house three hours to the north. I was granted unlimited visitation, but this made it very difficult. I have had a lot of failures in life. But I consider my failure to make my marriage work was my greatest of failures. Perhaps that's why I never remarried. Jo took everything we had acquired, but she let me keep the land and gingerbread house. I just wasn't sure what I was going to do with the land at that point. All my plans had lost their meaning.

That same year I was introduced to the daughter of an older couple I had done some work for. I had known Hellen and Warren Harris for about three years and didn't realize they had two daughters, Diane and Gracie. Gracie was married, she had two daughters and lived in Harrisburg Pennsylvania. Diane had never been married. She was a pretty blond, very intelligent and a hard-working career lady. She had a two-year degree in business and was running a sizable injection molding company. She was funny, fast-moving, and loved outdoor adventure. She took to my children like they were her own and we were a happy family.

In the winter of 1985, we found five acres on Church Road mid-way between Urbana, and Saint Parris. She told me exactly what she wanted in a house, and I built it for her. I spent the next two years landscaping the place. There was a small stream down the hill in back, and I built a covered bridge over it. I built a gazebo, a wishing well, a treehouse for the kids, and a place to watch the sunset. Although three of the five acres were wooded, I planted some decorative trees. I planted a small vineyard and I connected everything together with stone walks.

I turned thirty-two years old in 1986, and I had just about anything a man could hope for. I honestly couldn't think of anything I needed. When people told me, I should slow down and not work so hard, I just told them I was going to retire at forty. In my mind, I knew I would never retire, or even slow down at the age of forty. Why would I retire? I was keeping up with things. I took care of our place, some rental properties we owned, and I took care of Diane's parents' place.

One day I went out to cut the grass at their place, and Diane's mother said to me. "I like your new truck."

I said, "Yeah, but I'm getting a BMW. Is it all right to park it here for the night? I'll take it home tomorrow."

She gave me a really confused look and said, "Sure, I guess so." I had seen a manure spreader for sale along the road and I wanted it to plant flowers in. It was about ten miles away, and the steel wheels made a terrible racket as I pulled it behind my truck. Hellen and Warren were sitting in front of their garage when I rattled into their driveway. She asked, "What on earth is that you're pulling?"

I said, "It's a BMW, big manure wagon." I don't think I have ever seen two people laugh so much. I just looked at them with a puzzled expression and said, "What? I told you I was buying a BMW."

Hellen and Warren Harris were as dear to me as my own parents. I would sometimes sit for hours, just listening to their stories of the past. Hellen was born in Golden Valley Minnesota. Then her folks moved to Sioux Falls, South Dakota. She graduated high school there, then took a job for International Harvester in Montana. She was offered a pay increase if she would relocate to San Antonio Texas. One week later she boarded a south-bound train in Bozeman. The train was crowded with young men bound for basic training. The year was 1943.

She said she could still remember their faces. She described them as bold, daring, and so proud to go and fight for their country. She said it was sad to sit there and watch them, knowing that some of them would probably never see home again.

Warren was a local boy. He was born at a little crossroad place north of Springfield called Tremont City. He had worked as a janitor for a church before he was drafted into the army. He didn't see combat, but he served a year on the South Pacific island of New Caledonia. He was then transferred to Fort Sam, Houston Texas, near San Antonio, where he met Hellen. There were several black and white photographs taken that night on their first date. Two of the photos had been enlarged, framed and hung from the wall above the kitchen sink. They were like scenes from a Hollywood movie. Warren looked very much like Erol Flynn and Hellen looked like a pretty, blond, leading lady.

They were married in 1944. When Warren was discharged in 1945, they moved to Ohio. Warren went to work for International Harvester in Springfield. Hellen quit the plant when they decided to start a family. They bought ten acres of land about ten miles east of Springfield and Warren built a small house. They added on to the house as the years passed and their family grew. It never grew into a large house, but it was big enough for their comfort, and Warren built it with his own hands.

Warren was a true believer in the products he was helping to build at International Harvester. He drove a 1966 International pickup and mowed his yard with a

Cub-Cadet mower. Five of the ten acres were kept mowed. The trees were large oak and hickory, that provided shade for the entire yard. There was a row of tall Colorado blue spruce trees that were planted after they had been used as Christmas trees. Each tree slightly taller than the next, indicating the passing of years. The five acres in the rear of the property were fenced, and shaded by large oak and hickory trees as well.

There was an old barn near the center of that section. A barn, older than anyone knew. It was easy to see that those ten acres had been an oasis in the middle of a large farm. Oh, if that old barn could tell its story. I took a break from my chores on a bright summer afternoon. I found an old metal bucket behind the barn and took a seat on it. A breeze rocked the treetops just enough to allow the sun to shine on the spot where I was sitting. I leaned back against the warm back side of the barn. I'm not sure if I fell asleep, but I was so relaxed.

I didn't often take breaks from a busy day, but to steal away, relax, and daydream was one of my favorite things to do. I looked beyond the fence at the fields of corn, standing tall and green. Summer days were getting shorter now and I thought about how little time was left until harvest.

I saw what I thought were subtle changes in Hellen and Warren. And after seven years, those changes were not so subtle any more. Hellen was having a tough time getting in and out of vehicles, and Warren was having trouble remembering things. And you know, I was too arrogant to believe the same could happen to me one day.

To the north and west was a fifteen-hundred-acre farm that belonged to the Haddix family; Harvey, Ben, and Ed. All three had been professional baseball players when they were young. All three made the team for the Washington Senators. Ed and Ben became homesick for life on the farm. Harvey continued to play baseball for the senators until they moved to Minnesota and became the Twins. At that time, he became the starting pitcher for the Pittsburg Pirates. He retired from pitching, but he stayed on with the Pirates as a coach. I came to know Harvey about the same time I met Hellen and Warren (1981.) I guess I knew him more as a farmer than a baseball player, even though he wore two World Series rings. Harvey just wanted to complain about the weather and a late planting. He talked about whether or not the grain was ripe enough for harvesting.

Warren didn't mow the five acres in back, but he kept the fallen tree branches picked up. There were some tall weeds, but there were indelible pathways from the long years of livestock making their way to the barn at feeding time. Oh yes. What if that old barn could have talked? There was a concrete pad just outside the back door of the barn. It had a date pressed into it, but it had eroded and was no longer legible. In the center of the barn a ladder led to the hayloft. The steps of the ladder were worn from the many times it had been climbed. Sometimes climbed by the farmer, sometimes by children looking for a place to play.

It no longer had the smell of a barn, only the dry, musty smell of loneliness. Its outer walls and roof were covered with corrugated tin. But the tin was no longer shiny, just a faded gray. I loved that old barn as much as the Harris's. It just stood there like a silent partner, until a breeze brought a screeching moan to its eaves. The moan was no doubt created by a loose section of tin. But if you had in mind to nail down that loose section, you would never find it. It was there to speak.

Hellen and Warren loved each and every one of their neighbors, and each had his or her own unique story. The Vanhoose family lived just to the south and on the other side of the road. They were one of the largest egg farmers around. They supplied fresh eggs to grocery stores as far away as Columbus, Cincinnati, Dayton, and every mom and pop store in between. Then they were met with a string of bad luck. A fire destroyed two large barns killing thousands of chickens. Mister Vanhoose died in his late forties. Misses Vanhoose had worked for years as a model for JC Penny. I never met her, but I was told she was the most perfect woman in every way. However, she was killed in a plane crash in Tennessee. The farm was left to their son Darwin and daughter Vivilyn. Vivilyn became a model as well. She married a highway patrol officer and moved west of

Springfield. Darwin kept what was left of the egg business.

Just a little to the north and on the other side of the road was the home of Bobby and Judy Jones. Bobby bought ten acres of farmland from a large tract of land that belonged to Doctor Winterhawk. Doctor Winterhawk was a well-known physician whose practice included house calls in his younger days. He didn't sell his entire farm, just the ten acres where Bobby and Judy wanted to build their home.

Judy was Bobby's second wife. His first wife died giving birth to his second child David. Before he met Judy, Bobby lived through some tough and lonely years. Judy took to those children like they were her own. She did everything a young mother could do in her condition. You see, Judy could only walk with the aid of braces. Polio crippled her when she was a child.

Bobby had a battle with alcohol when his first wife died. But he ridded himself of those demons and became the most ambitious man I had ever known. He worked full time at Rockwell International, a company that produced aircraft beacons. He also worked part-time at Vining. Then he went to that ten acres of farmland and he started building a home for his family. I helped him when I could, and his brother-in-law helped him when he could. But for the most part, Bobby Jones built his home by himself. One little piece and one paycheck at a time. He knew it would take years, but when it was done it would be his own, and there would be no mortgage.

When he had finished the walkout basement, he installed a bathroom, three bedrooms and heated the whole thing with a wood-burning stove. Unfortunately, his project had to be placed on hold for almost two years when he was laid off at Rockwell. It was a sad looking affair, the basement his family lived in had a makeshift roof with a stovepipe sticking out of the top. I remember seeing the school bus stop to pick up the two children. They would appear from the rear of the basement and walk up the muddy embankment to get on the bus. Children at school called them, "The Mole People."

Another neighbor I remember was Doctor Runyon. He and his family lived almost a mile away near Clark Lake. In fact, the Runyon family had donated a large tract of land to the state of Ohio, that became Clark Lake State Park. Their home was a large two-story brick, built in the 1840s. He was from a long line of optometrists. His grandfather had traveled to Minnesota to intern with the famous Mayo brothers. William and Charles Mayo of the Mayo Clinic.

Hellen and Warren loved their neighbors and they were equally loved and respected. They had something growing in their yard from every neighbor. A fern, a Hosta, a potted plant, or a fruit tree. They would point to each plant or tree and tell the story of which neighbor gave it to them and when. It seemed that everything on their property had a story to tell.

Hellen and Warren lived a happy and wholesome life together. They even had a name for their little piece of the world. It was burned into a wooden plank that hung beneath the mailbox (Lazy Acres). They had lived the American dream, but I could see their cycle coming to an end.

One day a sheriff's deputy brought Warren home. Warren was driving on a country road a few miles from home when he pulled onto the side of the road. He was confused and unable to remember how to get home. He reluctantly gave up his keys when he was told he shouldn't drive. I didn't need it, but I bought his International pickup truck for eight hundred dollars. Warren became depressed. He would sometimes weep and ask, "What in the world is wrong with me?" Hellen became worried that he might hurt himself. She asked me to remove all the guns from their home. The time would come when Warren would spend as much as two weeks in the hospital and not remember it the next day. I think we all knew it, but no one was willing to say the words (Alzheimer's disease).

Chapter Twenty-Seven

A man would have to be completely stupid not to realize when he's happy. I could not think of one thing I wanted that I didn't already have. Diane and I were never married but we had five wondrous years together. We built a beautiful home on five acres tucked away at the end of a thousand-foot lane. The house was surrounded by woods on three sides. The woods ended about two hundred yards to the east. Beyond that was a large field. Except for one large white oak, the land to the west was fields of grain as far as you could see.

Like everyone, we built the house for entertaining guests. But we lived so far out in the country, we seldom had company. I built three covered porches. The patio ran all the way around the house. The front and back porches were covered with glass. I built a steel arch trellis which led to a large patio in front. There were two porch swings. One on the back porch and one on the porch facing east. The house featured skylights, a large stone fireplace, and cathedral ceilings. A spiral stairway led to a library on the balcony, which held several thousand books.

My business continued to grow. I had crews building new houses and crews working on remodels. Then I got to know a group of investors from Columbus. They were in the business of buying farms. My company was hired to remodel the houses and barns on those farms. The investors kept the land, but the houses and barns were sold as five-acre hobby farms.

I was making lots of money, but I was neglecting everything else in life. It got to the point when Diane and I seldom spoke, and when we did, the words were unkind. I only saw my children every other weekend. I had lost track of what was important in life.

One day in the spring of 1989, I told Diane I wanted to split up. I really didn't think she would care, but she was crushed. Shortly thereafter she moved out. She said she didn't want the house. It would just be too lonely living there alone. It wasn't until one lonely summer afternoon that I realized what a mistake I had made. I couldn't keep my mind on work, so I rented a movie and went home. I couldn't get interested in the movie either. I just sat on the couch staring down that long lane. In my mind, I could see her car coming up the lane and I was all ready to run out and greet her. I wanted to tell her to get packed for vacation. We would perhaps drive up to Niagara Falls or go to New York City for a few days. We would start a new life and learn to live again. But she never came home, it just wasn't her home any more.

I'm not sure I ever saw her again. She was married a year or so later. I kept the house, and it was every bit as lonely as she thought it would be. I worked until dark each day, and I just couldn't wait to get up and get out of there when morning came. But then I became accustomed to the loneliness, I think I became addicted to it. I developed agoraphobia. I didn't want to be in public.

There were two brothers who worked for me. Doug and David Lawson. Doug could do just about anything, and David had gone to vocational school for plumbing. I put the two of them in charge of my business. Those two were great, and they made it clear to everyone that I was to be left alone.

I went to work early and left around three-thirty. It was autumn and I just wanted to sit in the porch swing, watch the leaves fall and listen to the crickets. I watched the sunset and the breeze blowing across the cornfields. Then I would move to the back-porch swing. As the leaves fell I could see a little further each day. I could see beyond the woods, across the cornfields and the lights of Urbana. I watched the moon rise and just sat there mesmerized. I should have swept the leaves from the patio, but I guess I just didn't care anymore. Just after dark I would go inside and make a fire. I would read myself to sleep and wake up at three in the morning, forgetting every line I had read.

I lived there alone for almost three years until one day when my daughter visited. She said to me, "Dad, you know I love this house, but you spend too much time here alone. The happiness is gone. You should sell this place and get out of here. It's just not healthy for you." By the end of that week, I had put the house on the market.

I had dabbled in communications in the military. A friend in Columbus gave me a tip on a company called National Communications of Columbus. I hired on with them in March 1992. They were contracted to replace mainline overhead cables throughout Columbus for Warner Communications. I dissolved the construction business and decided to work an eight- or nine-hour day like the rest of the world. It was great, it was like the weight of the world was lifted from me.

The house sold within thirty days and I rented a small house in Columbus. National Communications was a nationwide company. My children were grown, and I was willing to travel for the company when the Columbus project was completed.

The work was new to me but very exciting. There were twenty-six of us in the crew I was working with. We used bucket trucks and ladders, but most of the climbing was done with gaffs. Or what some call climbing spurs. It was a beautiful spring and I loved the view from high atop those utility poles.

I got out of my truck one morning and met with Ralph White, the job foreman. He was all smiles. The kind of smile that makes one realize something's up. He said, "Good morning, Wynn. Can I have a word with you?"

I looked at him suspiciously and said, "Oh boy. Do I have a choice?"

He said, "Oh, it's not so bad. I have a proposition for you. I will give you a bonus if you'll train a man for me."

I said, "How much of a bonus and how long do I have to train him?"

He said, "One, six-day week. Anyway, I think you might know this guy."

We walked into the office and there was Mike Riley.

Before the day was over, Mike asked if he could "crash" at my place for a few days. It had been ten years, but I couldn't say no. I gave him a set of rules and he agreed. Mike hadn't changed much. He still liked to party, but he liked to do his partying on the town. We began to run together, and I must admit, we had a lot of fun. He liked to flirt with the girls, and his flirting almost got us into trouble one night. We were in a bar in the southside neighborhood of Grove City. Mike flirted with a group of girls, and one of them called him an old man. He said to me, "Wynn, I don't like this place. Let's take it down." He had his hand behind his back, holding a pistol that was stuck in his belt. I stopped Mike, and basically held him in his seat until I was able to talk him out of robbing the place. I like to think I kept Mike from doing something terrible that night.

He met a young girl who had an infant. When Mike didn't come home, I assumed he was with her. Mike fell into a group of people who were not exactly my type. I didn't see much of him after that, not even at work. I wasn't sure he still had a job with the company.

We emptied large wire spools and, like everyone else, I put one in the backyard for a picnic table. I was sitting at my makeshift table reading a book one Sunday afternoon when Mike showed up. He set a six-pack of cold Miller beer on the table and said, "Let's have a beer, man." We each opened a bottle, and Mike took a small sip, then set the bottle back in the carton.

I could tell something was troubling him. He didn't sit down, he lit a cigarette and asked, "Wynn, what happens to us when we die?"

I said, "I don't know, Mike. I like to think there's something for us."

He said, "I don't know about God, man, but I saw the Devil."

I put my book down and asked, "Where did you see the Devil, Mike?"

He said, "Lucasville Maximum Security Prison."

I don't remember the names in the story, but I remember the rest in detail. I'll just say Charlie was the bad guy and Joe was the victim. Mike didn't look at me as he was telling the story. He stared away into the distance. He had what we referred to in the Corps as the thousand-yard stare.

He said, "Charlie was on death row, man. So, he had nothing to lose. I don't know what Joe did to Charlie, but Charlie told everyone he was going to kill Joe. Everyone, that is, except Joe. We were out on the compound and Charlie was sitting on a tree stump. He had made himself a couple of shanks, man. Joe didn't know nothing, man. He just came walking by. Charlie waited till he passed. And Wynn, when Charlie came up off that stump, I saw the Devil. Everything about him changed. He was huge, and his face changed into something like I've never seen. He was like a werewolf or something.

"He went up behind Joe and he started sticking him. He was reaching over Joe's shoulders, stabbing him in the chest and ripping at his neck. Joe was trying to make it to the infirmary, but Charlie stayed on him. I don't know how Joe kept walking. It was just like you had taken a bucket of blood and poured it in a path behind them. Joe made it to the door of the infirmary and collapsed onto a handcart that was sitting just inside the door. He stopped moving, man, and we were all glad it was over. Charlie turned around, man, and the front of him was completely soaked in blood. Charlie walked back to the stump, dropped the shanks and sat back down. Then he began to look like a person again."

I didn't say anything, I didn't know what to say. I just started reading my book again. There was a fence row about twenty feet away, dividing my yard from the neighbors. There were bushes and assorted wild flowers growing along that fence. And the fence led to an alley. When I looked up from my book, Mike was looking at the flowers along the fence row. Each time I looked up, he was a little further away. It was as if he were studying every detail of every flower. The last time I looked up he was gone. The alley led to a neighborhood bar a block or so away. I thought perhaps he had gone there for a drink, or that someone had picked him up.

I never saw Mike after that. The next day at five a.m. on the 24th day of August 1992, Hurricane Andrew slammed into the coast of Florida, like a giant bulldozer blade. Florida Power and Light, and Bell South were desperate for help in restoring service. Just a few days later I was on my way. I didn't know it then, but I was embarking on the adventure of a lifetime.

End Notes

I guess I wish my life had been a little more predictable. I've always said, I've been blessed to be in the right place at the right time, and cursed to be in the wrong place at the worst time. I've written about so many people in this book. Many of whom are now sleeping peacefully in their graves. So many people whom I loved and respected. Vining closed its doors in 1999 and moved to Mexico. I'm sure it's safe to say that nearly every one of the Vining employees I wrote about in this book are gone. There are too many to mention, but I'll name a few of the people in this story who had the most impact on me.

Harvey Haddix always told me I needed to stop Warren from drinking. But Harvey was a chain smoker. Warren died in 1994 and Harvey died just one year later. Hellen died the day after Christmas 2004. Bobby and Judy Jones are both gone. Doctors Winterhawk, and Runyon both died in the early 90s.

I got a call from my former wife in the fall of 1993. Her brother Johnny had overdosed on heroin. He had been found unconscious and in the fetal position in the bathtub. He was so close to death; his vital organs had begun to shut down. He had laid on his right arm for so long it had to be amputated. If he was to live he would have to have a kidney transplant. I told the Riley family to list me as a donor. Miraculously, his kidneys began to function again, and a donor would not be needed. Johnny went straight after that, but he had to learn some new skills in order to make a living. He died on February 21st, 2008.

Mike was sent back to prison after I saw him in 1992. He was released in 2012 and moved in with his mother in Marysville. He was suffering with Chronic Obstructive Pulmonary Disease (COPD), I'm told he suffered horribly. In April 2013, Mike managed to get to his feet. He was confused when he walked out of his room where his entire family was waiting. He asked, "Man, what's going on? Am I dying or something?" A couple of hours later he was dead.

Death is a debt we all must pay. I'm sixty-three now, and death becomes more apparent each day. I suppose my life will end like most. It will end when someone walks out of a dismal room to an anxious group of friends or relatives and says, "It's over."